BY NONIE B. MCKINNEY

An International Bestseller

THINGS I LEARNED FROM WHITE FOLKS

Reporting Live From My Seat At The Table...

Table of Contents

Dear Readers,

Thank you for support. I just want to share a few things before you jump into this ocean of knowledge. I have very extreme views about religion, finance, family, the system, etc. Some of the things I say in this book might make you uncomfortable. That's good. Explore that. I'm sharing my personal experiences and interpretations of the lessons I'm learning about life. Everything else in this book can be researched.

*This is a book about gaining financial freedom by deprogramming and reprogramming your mind. It's also about Black people learning the importance of unity, breaking generational curses, buying Black, and group economics. It's time to learn some trade secrets that aren't taught in school and often times withheld specifically from Black people. I decided to call this book, "Things I Learned From White Folks" because in this country where we're all fighting for the "American Dream", they're living it- and the rest of us seem to be playing catch up. So I had to start paying attention and doing research. I'm not saying there aren't any black families already operating under these ideals, but it's not commonplace in our community. Many of you actually think success is "White Privilege", but part of it is really just— being informed. They just know the secrets and **The Secret**.*

Well, now you know it too. It's in your hands now.

It's time to change the narrative of people of color. Black people are community leaders. We are business owners. Our children are raised with love and are well-mannered. We are educated and our children are scholars. We are world travelers.

We are not underprivileged. "White Privilege" is an illusion. Now that I'm a "world citizen" I understand how pitiful and problematic it is to not understand or be "in the know" of the world around you.

I feel I'm a part of the Talented Tenth W.E.B. Du Bois talked about so it's my duty to come back and report what I learned when I got a seat at the table.

Love Always,

Nonie B.

P. S.

I would like to thank my fiancé for being an exceptional Black Man! A lot of this information stemmed from us just having late night conversations about life! That's beautiful because I've always wanted to be with a man who could teach me things. Thank you baby for being the type of man that believes in a strong Black Family Unit and a rich lineage (generational wealth).

I know that I'm two hands full, but you're so patient. I literally throw 1000 story ideas and business ideas at you each day and you remember like 3 of them. Hahaha! I love that about you! Don't change. Thank you for believing in me.

I love you...

Chapter 1: Knights at the Round Table

"Sticks in a bundle are unbreakable…"
~ African Proverb

In the black community we have been dealt a bad hand. *The Raw Deal*. We don't know our history. We've been programmed to hate ourselves, but then idolize cultural appropriation and actually buy back our *own* beauty standards. Most of us even believe we are descendants of slaves out of Africa and that we are living in a foreign country. Many Black people even worship a white god. Not realizing, subconsciously you're being programmed to see the white man as *"Supreme"*. I may not have enough time in this self-help manual to deprogram and reprogram a whole community, but I can tell you where to start. It all starts in our minds.

I was stuck just like you, but then a lightbulb went off. Like the old saying goes, "Fool me once, shame on you; fool me twice, shame on me". I started paying attention. I started noticing patterns. The first one I caught myself falling into was the "broke mindset". I'll never forget the first time a bill collector called my phone and my first response (automatic) was to yell into the phone, "YOU'LL GET IT WHEN I GET IT" and quickly hang up! It was shocking because it's something my mother always did. Her signature, if you will. I caught it. I had been programmed to be broke(n). But I was determined to fix it. I did. So I know you can too.

Some look at white people as having privilege. Privilege. Noun. A special right, advantage, or immunity granted or available only to a particular person or group of people. It's true. You can check the "Criming While White" hashtag on any social media platform and read countless stories of white people abusing their "privilege". But we can't get mad. We have to get knowledgeable then we have to get *active*.

You have to first understand there is no "White Privilege" without *"Black Compliance"*! For the duration of this book we won't look at "privilege" as what people are "allowed to do," but instead let's look at it for what it is — what *people are "knowledgeable about"*.

In this book we will explore key tools I learned from looking over white folks' shoulders and how we can apply them and finally get ahead of **the game**. I'm going to use a series of comparisons to help you understand how the other side accomplishes and maintains *"The American Dream"* **and how you can too.**

Headstart

Nepotism. Noun. The practice among those with power or influence of favoring relatives or friends, especially by giving them jobs.

This key tool is number one for a reason. It's the main ingredient for white people's success. They keep it all in the family (and no that's not a redneck joke— close). It dates as far back as the days of Kings and Queens. Royalty would marry and breed with relatives to keep royalty within the family. The same exists today with jobs and power. "It's not what you know; it's who you know"!

Donald Trump is the perfect example of nepotism. His daughter, son, and son-in-law now have political positions. His cabinet (once upon a time) was filled with his closest friends, including reality TV star Omarosa
(who's job description and duties have never been uncovered).

They've been doing this for so long that they have a head start. When we think about successful white people we assume they came from a two parent, two income, educated household. But we never think about the grandfather and his father and his father. They all had insurance to make sure once they were gone, their families would be straight. While we, on the other hand, are taught, *"You can't take it with you"*. You're not supposed to Black People! You're supposed to continue the empire which means you have to build one, first. Your bloodline is supposed to run long and be *rich.*

They pass down net worth and network, making sure their bloodlines always have something to bring to the table.

The Round Table

My fiancé named this chapter and asked if I'd ever heard of King Arthur. Of course I had, but then he asked, *"Do you know why the table is round?"* No. "So that there's not one particular person in charge, everyone plays an important part!"

That stuck out to me because I've seen that round table in so many other movies with white actors, but in New Jack City, Nino Brown had a long rectangular table that he sat at the head of. I'm just saying. It makes sense. In the black community we have far too many chiefs and not enough Indians. Everyone so ready to be a boss that they forget you must acquire certain skill sets first.

I know this guy who's been building cars since he was in high school. Great guy and talented, but couldn't get out his own way. One time something was wrong with his girlfriend's car. She'd taken it to several mechanics that told her to take it to the dealership. She took it to the dealership. He called to check on it at the dealership and they couldn't figure it out either. So he went down there to look at it. He fixed it. Simple. The manager was in such awe that he offered him a job on the spot! He said in all of his 14 years at the company (luxury car dealer) he'd never seen that type of skill. Don't you know he cursed the man out and left! He felt insulted to be offered a job to work under someone. He feels he should have his own shop. He should! But how will he ever get there if he doesn't take the necessary steps? He could have taken that job and pulled a few customers over to the side for cheaper prices if he worked on them at home. Working at the dealership alone builds clientele. He could have done anything, but he did nothing and many of you are just like that.

Take my family for instance. I've been in the entertainment industry for over a decade now and most of us have an affinity for the arts. We could have started a label by now and put out our own projects. It's just this weird thing about wanting to be *"The One"* so instead of working together they'd rather struggle. No one wins when the family feuds...

The Token Black vs. The Talented Tenth

This need to be "The One" or "The First One" or "The Only One" is holding us back by keeping us apart. I'm actually the type of person who loves to share knowledge and if I have contacts then I'll share them too. But we all know that a large majority of you try to harbor all the money, knowledge, and contacts. It's sad. "I'm the only black at the office!" I remember hearing people make statements like that with the biggest grins on their faces. The listeners were no better because they gloated as if it's some type of accomplishment. It's not. In fact, that example should go in reverse and it could if we get it together.

I'll never forget the time I walked onto a set and saw that my fellow "sista" was the boss! I was super excited like, **"Come thru sis!"** That excitement went away when I realized she was in charge of hiring, yet she never called me, but the white girl did. Yes, you read that right! A white chick (entry level) got me the gig. My own "sista" (upper level) didn't call me. Then one day at lunch while we were just chatting I guess her guilty conscience couldn't take it cause she was like,

"I be trying to put my people on, but you know you can't have too many of us in one place. Not with my name on it." That shit really pissed me off. At the end of the day, that's your civic duty to put "your kinfolk and your skin folk" on. That's what they do! And they don't care about their name getting dirty.

Bob could have a son named Robbie who's a drug addict that needs a job. Bob will talk to Steve like, "Yea, Robbie's trying to clean up his act. You got any work for him?" Bruh. He knows Robbie might not even show up the first day, but he's reppin' for him!

It's a got damn shame that my fiancé's dad worked for a company for 37 years making six figures and not once did he put his son on. His son never asked and he never thought about it. If that were a white man and his son didn't have plans of going to college, he would have had him on that job straight out of high school. We have to get into the habit of taking care of our people, especially our children. At least, help where you can.

Ninety percent of you don't want the information because you don't want to feel obligated to apply it. The other 10% get their money and move away. They don't throw back so much as a crumb to the community. Meanwhile, white people are out here volunteering at Habitat For Humanity and rebuilding rundown homes in our neighborhoods. But I can't even stress the importance of giving back until I get you to move forward.

Conspectus

Let me remind you that there are fundamental differences between blacks and whites that we must embrace. With every thing that I've said, don't take it as a Black vs. White "thing" and convince yourself that I'm downing my people or worse— being racist. I'm not. I'm talking about my own personal experiences since I'm someone who you would say has "made it"! Now I'm telling you how. We would have all the same values that take you higher had we not gone through slavery which systematically and mentally broke us down. It's time to take back the pride, family values, and dreams that our ancestors attempted to instill in us. We owe that to the next generations.

One time I had a long talk with my friend Tiffy who lives in Rancho Cucamonga, California. Yes, I know. I thought it was just something Ice Cube made up at first too. But she let me know she had worn her natural hair all summer because her daughter was hurt that a student made an insensitive comment about her hair. "Crazy hair day was yesterday!" My friend's daughter is a black girl with a big curly afro. She's one of maybe 3 blacks in the class. That's heart wrenching, but the conversation went further.

I often times boast online about being a black woman and never wanting to be anything else. I often boast about growing up in New Orleans, a majority black city that is run BY BLACKS! I also went to college in Atlanta, Georgia, a majority black city RUN BY BLACKS! Both currently have a Black Woman as mayor, Latoya Cantrell (NOLA) and Keisha Lance Bottoms (ATL). It's a beautiful thing and I love Black People! Tiffy commented, "I've been thinking about your experiences and all your success. I think it may have something to do with growing up around blacks. Here in California we aren't #1. We are 3#. The whites are the head then the Mexicans run everything and act like the white folks (in terms of systematic oppression of blacks). When you talk about your grandfather being a business owner for over 30 years and your grandmother working for the city I think about all the obstacles that I've faced and how I didn't grow up thinking I could do anything like that. Now I feel like I'm at a major disadvantage by not having that support. When you live so closely with whites you encounter the oppression directly."

I'd never thought about it like that because I can count on one hand how many white people I actually know personally. But I've worked with them. Sometimes it feels like that's all I work with— others. So I'm telling you the shit I learned from them and how to apply it.

But here's a little story of how black people have used Nepotism in the right way.

I was watching an Eddie Griffin interview and he told the story about how the box office hit, *"Foolish"* came about. He said in maybe 1992 he had a comedy show at the Saenger Theater in New Orleans. The promoters came to his dressing room and told him some local artists wanted to know if they could open up for him. He said, "Send them back and let me hear if they can spit!" Master P and Mystikal came to the back and did a lil something. He liked it and let them open the show! They killed it and **No Limit Records** took off. He said in 1998 Master P came to a show to see him. He entered the green room and told Eddie, "You probably don't remember me!" Eddie said, "Yea, I remember you." By that time Master P was the best thing smoking! So Master P said, "Well since you did that for me in '92 and put me on, I want to do something for you." He asked Eddie if he had any scripts. Eddie said he sped home and edited some pages and brought a script back to Master P who turned around and gave him $1 million-of *his own money!* The independent movie dropped in September of 1999 and made over $6 million![1]

That's not only how Karma works. Baby that's NEPOTISM at it's finest! We need to make it a way of life!

Chapter 2:
Nobody Wins When The Family Feuds

*"When brothers fight to the death, a stranger
inherits their father's estate."*
~ Ibo Proverb

White picket fence. 2 ½ kids. Upper middle class 3
bedroom home. Insert last name on the mailbox.

Two parents.

Let that all sink in. They sold us the dream a long time
ago, but the blueprint for the hustle was sold separately.
The Cosby Show was our answer to that.

None of this may seem like a big deal because most of
us didn't have a childhood remotely close to this and we
came out ok, right?

Right.

But do you feel like you missed out on something?

Well, you probably did. Especially if you grew up in a
single parent household, or with your grandparent(s) - in
public housing or on government assistance. It all plays a
part. Many of the issues we face today actually come from
a void built by not having basic necessities.

What's Missing?

Two parents.

White people believe in marriage (I said nothing about
its sanctity or longevity). White people recognize that their
family is their strength in any situation so they lead with
that. It looks good on paper. Married people "appear" more

responsible. It's more "classy" than shacking up. For white men it's important to pass on their lineage. None of them want to give their last names to an illegitimate child. That's why most white children in single parent white homes don't even know who their fathers are if he was never married to their mothers. The women are scared to shame the alleged father's family name with a "bastard".

They instill in their children to marry in their 20's, preferably after college. Take the name and part of your inheritance and go out and take over the world. Procreate so we can carry on our bloodline and all its history. They understand the importance of the children being brought up right to carry on the legacy.

Hell, in the black community we can barely get past our maternal grandparents on a family tree. You can walk into a white "family home" right now today in 2018 and see a painting of an ancestor of theirs' from 1785 who went to school with George Washington. Family is everything to them, especially if they have a lil money.

We can barely go to the park for a reunion with our family without some dumb shit "poppin off" cause somebody said the macaroni was dry.

I was just reading an article that said, 64 percent of all children live with married parents. I was like- DAMN! THAT'S HIGH! THEY BUGGIN! But then I read it's been on a steady decline since 1960 when it was 88 percent.

But don't get the game twisted. Most white people I have come across— grew up in a single parent home or with a step parent. Where do you think child support comes from? They always take care of their own first! Remember that. The system was already in place because white men would run off on their kids. The media would have you believe it's a "Black Thing". No honey! In fact, CDC studies show that Black Men are more involved with their children than any other race— even when they don't live in the home! But we wouldn't know that because the stereotype is creating an illusion. We need to step up and reclaim family ties! We have to show the youth it can be done because it's being done. But we have to bring the BLACK FAMILY UNIT BACK!

Research also shows that family intactness has a beneficial influence on reducing out of wedlock births, increasing high school and college graduation rates, and even has long-term benefits such as higher employment rates. That's because, in two parent families, children typically have access to more of the economic and community resources because parents are able to pool their time, money and energy; children tend to be more of the focus of the home.[2] But that's understandable. Two heads are usually better than one. Two incomes as well.

Family Inheritance

An inheritance is something you receive from the previous generation. It could be good looks and a charismatic persona (genetic makeup), money, land, property... or **DEBT**. I'm not gonna act like we didn't make the list black people. We have a great genetic makeup. That's why we rule in all sports. Yes, even baseball. The Dominicans are killing it and they identify as people of color or brown people. Now a Black Man is taking over hockey. We look good. We are very creative and innovative. But white folks inherit land, money, and property. And in this game, you need that.

I was talking to my Armenian friend one day and she told me a story from her childhood. Her uncle, a wealthy man, used to make her cousins (his son and daughter) treat a penny like a pet when they were kids. They had to take that penny for a walk. They had to have in depth conversations with their pennies. The pennies went wherever they went. Each child had to sleep with the penny somewhere close at night. She said she thought he was crazy, as did her cousins, but now at almost 30— **WE ALL UNDERSTAND IT**. He was grooming his kids to maintain the family's money. After all, it's a part of the family.

What do we do?

Chile, if I had a penny for every time my mom's furniture was almost repo'd by Rent-A-Center when I was a kid, for every eviction notice and every time the utilities (power and water) were cut off, for the times the cable got cut off and the bills were late, I'd be rich. But we used to be dressed to impress. She bought a "tax time car" every year. Honey I know about it. ***Robbing Peter to pay Paul*** was my mom's "go-to". It's like a Super Power within black households! Who do I need to pay this week, how much do I need for me and my kids to survive the week, and who can actually wait for their payment without my services being interrupted? My mom was no Einstein so she failed at that miserably.

> It's draining. So if you lived like that as a kid and you're still living like that now as an adult— I'll just say I'm glad you bought the book.

But something hit me after I realized I was on a downward spiral when it comes to this slippery slope of poverty. I started to recognize the patterns. I'd been on my own for a while so I had experience with paying bills and… not paying bills. Collections companies started calling me too. My credit was fucked up. No, I wasn't as bad off as others, but I was headed there. No one had ever sat down with me and explained how things go and how money works. Clearly they were not privy to the information because no one had taught them either. It's not taught in schools. That would be too much like right, to actually teach us some useful information. I still haven't had to do any trigonometry since I left high school.

Money Management would have been a better course. Most of our families don't know how to handle money because they never had any. But that goes back to the story about building a relationship with money. We are subconsciously taught to live in poverty.

But you can break out of that with these few keys that you've heard before, but never grasped their importance.

1. When you apply to rent an apartment, the combined income of the household must be 3 times higher than the rent. Why? Because logically and mathematically speaking, if the rent is $500 and you don't make at least $1500/month then you can't afford to live there once you factor in a car note, insurance, utilities, cable, going out, etc. But black people will make $1500/month and get a $800 apartment, $300 car note, $150 car insurance, utilities and cable equalling $500 and still want to spend $200 every weekend and wonder why they have to get a pay day loan every Friday and the furniture is about to get repo'd even though the bill is only $45/month. It's simple math.

2. IF you can't buy 2 of them, you can't afford it. If you have $500 in your account and the purse is $300— you can't afford that purse. Black people think the object of the game is to spend all their money. It's not. The object of the game is to live comfortably and in peace. It's completely ok to save up for something because you're moving money to the side over a period of time, not throwing away a lump sum. Hopefully your other responsibilities are in order before you start making major purchases.

3. If you can't buy it CASH you can't afford it. YES! Credit is EVERYTHING! But too many people (all races) get caught in the vicious cycle of credit card debt. Credit is a back up plan. It's a safety net. If a tightrope walker fell into the safety net at the bottom all the time, the show would be a bust. The number one complaint would be, *"If she needs the safety net so much maybe she doesn't know what she's doing. She needs more training."* Same goes for credit cards. If you're always using your credit card to bail you out maybe you need to go back to the drawing board and re-assess your income versus expenses.

We don't talk about money open and honestly in the black community and we need to. It's time to get educated about money and break the cycle of poverty.   J. Cole said it best in his song *"Money"* from the **"Born Sinner"** album:

> *How mama gonna teach you how to save yo money*
> *When she barely on the boat got stay afloat money*
> *Blacks always broke cause we don't know money*
> *Spend it before we get it and could never hold money*
> *No wallets, nah, ~~nigga~~ we'd rather fold money*
> *Money control ~~niggas~~, white man control money*
> *Laughing like "yeah yeah… my ~~nigga~~ get yo money[3]*

Family Secrets

Mental Health is another thing we don't talk about in the black community. Mental illness is running rampant through the hood. So many are clinically insane and have never been diagnosed. But to make it out of what most of us come from, in your right mind, is a rarity.

White children are not consistently exposed to emotional trauma. That makes all the difference in the world. Pre-exposure to adversity changes the DNA.

Dr. Nadine Burke Harris puts it best:

"We now understand better than we ever have before how exposure to early adversity affects the developing brains and bodies of children. It affects areas like… the pleasure and reward center of the brain that is implicated in substance dependence. It inhibits the prefrontal cortex, which is necessary for impulse control, an executive function, a critical area for learning. And on MRI scans, we see measurable differences in the amygdala, the brain's fear response center.

So there are real neurologic reasons why folks who are exposed to high doses of adversity are more likely to engage in high-risk behavior. And that's important to know. But it turns out that even if you don't engage in any high-risk behavior, you're still more likely to develop heart disease or cancer. The reason for this has to do with the hypothalamic-pituitary-adrenal axis, the brain's and body's stress response system that governs our fight-or-flight response. How does it work?

Well, imagine you're walking in the forest, and you see a bear. Immediately, your hypothalamus sends a signal to your pituitary, which sends a signal to your adrenal gland that says, release stress hormones adrenaline, cortisol. And so your heart starts to pound. Your pupils dilate. Your airways open up. And you are ready to either fight that bear or run from the bear. And that is wonderful if you're in a forest, and there's a bear. But the problem is what happens when the bear comes home every night. And this system is activated over and over and over again.

And it goes from being adaptive or lifesaving to maladaptive or health-damaging. Children are especially sensitive to this repeated stress activation because their brains and bodies are just developing. High doses of adversity not only affect brain structure and function, they affect the developing immune system, developing hormonal systems and even the way our DNA is read and transcribed."[4]

She went on to say, *"Some kids who demonstrate behavioral symptoms, as adults are more likely to suffer from depression, attempt suicide, have problems in the workplace, and become incarcerated. But some kids don't show any behavioral symptoms. Some kids just get sick all the time - rashes or asthma or auto-immune disease - right?* - where your immune system attacks your own body, right?" And I know that to be true because I have experienced both sides of the coin.

This is what our children inherit and this has to stop. On top of that, most of us who grew up in the 90's are the off spring of drug users from the crack epidemic in the 80's. Studies show that children of substance abusers are 3 times as likely to abuse drugs and alcohol as well. This is another reason for high crime in the hood. Lack of jobs and resources is the reason, but the emotional response to this oppression hinders us further. We go through all of this shit before high school and are expected to be productive. It's almost impossible. But somehow we must.

Meanwhile, in the white community, 40 year old Brad still lives in the basement and is waited on hand and foot, probably still gets an allowance.

I was talking to a Middle Eastern car salesman in California one day. He was around 60 years old and he was tired. He had 3 grown sons that still lived at home. I asked if he was ready for them to go. He said, "Well one (30) was just there while he waited to close on his house with his wife. The two younger ones (26 and 28) are pooling their money together to franchise a Chick-Fil-A. So I guess it all paid off."

Most of us ran away from home a few times and couldn't wait to turn 18 so we could leave or be kicked out. Some of us left or were kicked out far before 18. There's a clear disconnect. African Proverbs call children **"the reward of life"**. You're supposed to build them up to be better than you. We don't do that, but we need to start.

Family Business

Planning for the future is the white family's favorite thing to do. They already have a 5-10 year plan and insurance to protect that plan. We don't even have insurance when we die. That's why I was surprised when my fiancé had an IRA and 401k and all kinds of shit I just considered *"Shit White Folks Do"!* They handle the family business. If someone dies there's a $100,000 insurance policy, a $300 cremation, and the family invests whatever money is left after closing out that person's bills. In the black community, there is no insurance. If your ass dies we sell $7 fish plates and shirts to pay for a $10,000 funeral equipped with a live band, horse and carriage, a banquet buffet, a life size cut out of you, and some Versace so the deceased can be "FRESH TO DEATH"! Hilarious!

I personally love that GHETTO SHIT! But it's not right. *Post Traumatic Slave Syndrome* has done a number on us. And we insist on passing it down to future generations, furthering mental bondage. Do white families have issues? Yes. They go to therapy. Therapy? Yes! I said therapy! We need to understand that seeking help doesn't make us crazy! Not acknowledging we need help and living the same drama and trauma over and over again makes a person crazy. We need to start sitting down at the dinner table with our kids again as a way of debriefing about the day. It's time to take our well being into our own hands.

No more deep dark secrets and family shame. Yes, we grew up with less than average. Yes, some of us have been abused by family members and family friends. Yes, some of us have no clue how to survive outside of government assistance. But it's time to get real. Research. Talk to people who seem to be doing better than you.

Even with everything that happened with my first "family business", I haven't given up on the idea of working with my siblings and cousins. I won't allow one rotten apple to spoil the bunch, but I can't lie, I'm apprehensive. But I know where I went wrong. It's okay to work with family and friends, but they also have to come to the table with something, even if it's just a proven track record. People like me always want to "take everybody with me" and not everyone can go. You have to treat a family business just like any other company. If they don't qualify to work there… they don't qualify.

Wal-Mart is a family owned business.

Volkswagen, Ford, Koch, and Dell Technologies all fall under the category of FAMILY BUSINESS.

You and your family can have a business that is successful, be it a lil moms and pops joint or a major corporation. Don't give up!

Conspectus

In that presentation by Dr. Nadine Burke Harris she goes on to say those harsh conditions our children face lead to dispositions such as *"failure to thrive"*. Remember in Chapter 1 when I told you about the guy who could build cars as a teen, but never took off? Well, he lived in a home where his father constantly told him he would never be anything and til this day he hasn't done much. When I was a kid my grandfather told my grandmother (in front of me), "She ain't gon be nothing but a crack hoe like her mama"!

That stuck with me. I wanted to beat his ass! So I decided to beat him at his own game. I'll never let a person say something negative about me and be proven right. I'm a major success! I grew up and became *"The American Dream"*. I have a college degree, I followed my dreams! I work in my field. I worked at the #1 Urban Radio Station in the country, then moved into freelance television production. I've done production on some of your favorite movies and television shows. I'm a tax paying business owner. I don't have any children "out of wedlock" and I recently got engaged to my best friend. I'm not even 30 years old yet and you're reading my book. White folks out here ain't even pulling that off no more. I did it the *"right"* way and now I'm teaching you to do the same! It doesn't matter if you haven't accumulated the same success. It doesn't matter if you've done everything *"wrong"*. You could have done absolutely nothing at all. But that stops with this book. It's time to turn the page!

Jay-Z said it best, "We lose cause we never had the tools. I'm tryna fix ya! I'm tryna get these ~~niggas~~ with no stripes to be official."

1.   We must first identify the problems we have within ourselves then within our family units. Whether it's substance abuse, the living paycheck-to-paycheck mindset, or just bitter from deep dark family secrets that you haven't been able to release. It's time to seek help. It's time to be victorious over your trials and tribulations.

2.   We must be more compassionate and nurturing towards our children because they are our gifts. Stop giving them adults troubles like— raising their siblings, or worrying about bills and where their next meal is going to come from. Stop kicking them out without fully raising them.

3.   Make a plan. Insure it. Move towards it like it's
        your only option.

Time to build a better and stronger family structure. If
we could come together like we do with the electric slide
when that Frankie Beverly and Maze *"Before I Let Go"*
comes on-WE **WOULD BE UNSTOPPABLE!**

Chapter 3: Health is Wealth

"What is in the stomach carries what is in the head."
~ Kenyan Proverb

We laugh.

"White folks can't cook. They don't season their food!"

They don't.

Their food is horrible.

But so is ours.

Macaroni and cheese, collard greens, dumplings, smothered pork chops, potato salad, rack of ribs, fried chicken and mashed potatoes with gravy.

Soul Food.

It's good for the souls of black folks, but not good for our hearts, minds, and bodies.

Diabetes, hypertension, and heart disease are not hereditary, but chitterlings, pork chops, and ham hocks are! There's absolutely nothing hereditary about dying from high cholesterol at age 40! It's solely dietary.

Smoothies and Salads vs. Soul Food

Let's break it down. White people don't eat soul food. Why not? Because they can't cook! Hahaha! No, but seriously, they eat REAL FOOD! They eat a lot of fruits and vegetables. They eat salads and drink smoothies. I was always baffled by this because I figured, well if we were cooking for them, they must have at one point been eating what we were eating.

Au de Contraire.

3 words.

Slave Quarters Special.

During slavery, "Massa" used Aborigine people to tend to the crops and animals, but would not allow us to eat off the fat of the land. We were thrown the scraps of the animals. That's where the affinity for ribs, pig feet, chitterlings aka chittlins', pig lips, neck bones, etc., comes from.

We fry it in lard/grease which is nothing but animal fat. Then here comes the salt!!!

Seasoning is not bad, don't get me wrong. You should season your food. If you adopt a plant based diet you wouldn't have to worry about that too much. That's the best route to take, but if you insist on eating dead animal carcass you should use all natural seasoning— fresh oregano, parsley, onion, garlic, etc. That's located in the "produce section". That's what I do as I struggle to keep my 80% plant based regimen going.

We consume a lot of sodas and junk food. We drink a lot of liquor never thinking of the many calories it holds. What about genetically modified foods? GMO foods are produced from organisms that have had changes introduced into their DNA using the methods of genetic engineering. And what do you think happens when you eat food who's DNA has been genetically modified? Your DNA changes. Watch *"What The Health"* and you may never eat again.

I watched a video about a guy who worked in the meat department of a grocery store for 5 years. He said sometimes they would find cancerous tumors in the meat and just cut it out and continue on with the order. They also took old meat and dipped it in blood to give it a fresh look as they changed the expiration date. Have you seen some of these slaughter houses? Rat infested.

These are the chances we take everyday when eating something as simple as a burger and fries. It's time to start rethinking our diets.

Here are a few things you could do to switch it up:

1. Drink more water. Some of you think water tastes nasty. *Side eye*. I'm baffled. But that's fine because fruit infused water is just as tasty as a juice. Hot lemon water in the morning jump starts your metabolism for the day. Make sure you drink 2 liters of water each day.

2. Monitor your portions. Heavy breakfast. Medium lunch. Light dinner.

3. Don't eat after 8pm. All food needs to be fully digested before you go to bed.

4. If you're a late night snack kind of person like I am, eat almonds or blueberries. They shave belly fat. You can also have yogurt and granola.

5. No GMO. Look at the numbers on your produce. Five numbers, starting with "8", means it was genetically modified. Four numbers, starting with "4", means it was grown conventionally (but may still have pesticides on it). Five numbers, starting with "9" means it's organic. If it starts with "3" or says "seedless" it's not meant for you.

I know what you all are thinking, "We all gotta die someday." My answer is— Yes, but not every day. That food not only alters your body, it alters your mood and affects your health. This is the difference between living 20 years longer and looking at least 20 years younger. If nothing else, **MAKE SURE YOU EXERCISE**.

Namaste

When you think of exercise you either get a moving image of a muscle bound white man going hard and yelling, "Feel The Burn"! Or you might think of 3 white ladies power walking in a quiet, affluent neighborhood. But I want you to think about Yoga. Not white ladies holding yoga mats— **YOU** sitting with your legs crossed aka "Indian style" with your eyes closed. ***Ohm***. Yoga is a group of physical, mental, and spiritual practices and disciplines. I love it because it has a meditative and spiritual core, it's not just physical exercise.

For beginners, it gets you to focus on your breathing and being *"in the now"*. The stillness helps reduce stress and assists with relaxation. It's low impact so you can do it even if you have old injuries. You're also working against your own body weight so you won't necessarily hurt yourself if you are overweight or haven't worked out in a while.[5]

I named this subchapter "Namaste" because it means, *"The good in me recognizes the good in you"*. It's a really spiritual moment between two people who have meditated and moved spiritually together in a yoga session.

Health is about a lot more than food. We've already talked about mental and emotional issues. Meditating can help. Get your spirit right because fixing the inside magically fixes the outside.

You can start making a mental transformation and preparing yourself for yoga by practicing affirmations. Affirmations are sentences aimed to affect the conscious and the subconscious mind. The words composing the affirmation, automatically and involuntarily, bring up related mental images into the mind, which could inspire, energize and motivate. Repeating affirmations, and the resultant mental images, affect the subconscious mind, which in turn, influences the behavior, habits, actions and reactions.[6] So in short, think positive and visualize positive images to accompany the thought.

Try this 21 Day Affirmation challenge from
DailyCupOfYoga.com:

21 DAYS of AFFIRMATIONS

1.   I am peaceful and calm.
2.   I always deserve love.
3.   I trust myself.
4.   I attract amazing people.
5.   I love and approve of myself.
6.   I am happy in my own skin.
7.   The past has no power over me anymore.
8.   I feel good about myself.
9.   I am open to receiving love.
10.   I attract loving, beautiful people into my life.
11.   I accept myself exactly as I am.
12.   I am grounded in acceptance.
13.   I am grateful.
14.   Others love me easily and joyfully.
15.   I am never alone.
16.   I express love freely.
17.   I create my life and no else makes it for me.
18.   I am a radiant being filled with light and love.
19.   I attract loving relationships into my life.
20.   I am healthy and strong.
21.   I turn my dreams into reality.

Pick one of these each day for the next 21 days and say
it to yourself all day long, write it down, email it to
yourself, post it up on your mirror. Surround yourself with
the positive vibration of each affirmation one day at a time.
See for yourself that affirmations are what yoga talks about
in harnessing the power of our intentions and directing
them in the direction of our best selves and our happiest
lives.[7]

Social Networks

Another thing we need to do is UNPLUG! Everything we do now is connected to electricity and the internet. No more books. No more quiet time. No more living a full day and going home to listen to messages on the answering machines. Radiation is at an all time high with microwave dinners and "antennas" on every device we use. We even sleep with these things in bed with us at night or on the night stand next to the bed. That's too close for comfort. We sleep with radio active frequencies bouncing off our brains and organs. Think about that.

But aside from possible brain cancer, social media can be toxic in general. You have millions of people digitally uploading every intimate detail about their lives. The sad part is… depending on who you follow, 80 percent of the shit that comes down your timeline is garbage, lies, and negativity. People whining about infidelity. People uploading live fights. Trolls arguing in the comment section. Turn it off! **SHUT OUT THE NOISE!** It's not good for the mind and spirit. On social media I follow "the woke community". I follow travel pages, chefs, yoga pages, meditation pages, brujas and other spiritual healers, money management pages, and anything else that lines up with how I view myself and the life I want.

I don't follow celebs and "reality TV stars" because it's too dramatic and that's not what I want for my life. I follow close friends and family. I've also unfollowed many of them who were posting nothing but bullshit all day.

You are responsible for your own health: mental, emotional, and physical so it's definitely okay to block out anything that doesn't feed your spirit positively.

Conspectus

Health is wealth. Stop spending so much time obsessing about the outside. Stop trying to be perfect for the world. What really matters most is what is within. Are you happy with yourself?

We need to change the idea of soul food. Soul Food should nourish the mind, body, and spirit. Let's get healthy!

Stories have been told of many people curing all diseases in their body just by changing what they eat.

It's important to get accustomed to cleansing and detoxifying, be it from food, or from foolery. Release those toxins.

Get quiet. Get still. Breathe. Let it go.

Look in the mirror and say 3 things you love about yourself. Write it down.

Realize that you are co-creating your life with God and everything you give emotion to, you attract more of. So make sure that whatever you give your thoughts and energy to is what you really want. Make sure it's positive.

And in your free time you should read *"The Secret"* to get ready for my next book.

Chapter 4: Act As If

"Fake it til you make it!" ~ Unknown

I was so hesitant to use that quote. "Fake it til you make it"! Why? Because black people take it way too far. Haha! *Acting as if* you have a million dollars and "*spending a lot of money on random bullshit*" are **not the same**. Let me be clear.

So what is "acting as if"?

Well, let's see how I can put this.

You know THAT ONE co-worker "who thinks they're the manager"? Yes! We've all had that co-worker and more often than not that person is WHITE! Hilarious! But there's something to it. That co-worker is "acting as if" (s)he is the manger because that is the desire. That is the plan! That is what's NEXT!

Black people do it all wrong. I'll give you an example, I was doing press for a red carpet event and overheard some chicks talking. One was saying she'd decided to buy an $800 dress instead of paying her rent for her studio apartment with the air mattress on the floor. That's absolutely ridiculous and that plays into the "poverty mindset"! If you can't buy a $25 dress and make it look like a million bucks you ain't winning!

Just like all the young black males who are "acting as if" they are multi-platinum selling recording artists. What are they doing? Most are in "studio sessions" all the time—high. They spend their days smoking, drinking, and chasing hoes. I mean, ain't that what the rappers do in the music videos?

That's not "acting as if"! That's acting an ass!

Yes! That's what's done in the videos after they're superstars! They had to grind and put in work before that. If you were acting as if, you'd be making hits and doing shows— building your name.

Did THAT ONE co-worker go out and buy an expensive suit to act as the manager? No. He simply assumed the role and played the part consistently. That's why they always go on to manage something somewhere. If Petty Cash Wop (I made that up lol) went into the studio and consistently made good music like the hottest rappers, he could win. Desiigner. Future.

The end.

Fluff Your Resume

Now allow me to break down how white people do it.

Before I became a successful entrepreneur I was subject to the boring interviews and the dreadful resume changes. Glad that's over. But if you're still there, it's time to get a clue— **MAXIMIZE YOUR POTENTIAL!**

For example, let's say your caucasian counterpart works with you at the tax office dressed as Lady Liberty. When tax time is over, your resume will say "Tax Office Sign Waver/Mascot". Your caucasian counterpart's resume will simply read— "Marketing Affiliate"! Do you see how that could lead you two down completely different paths and ultimately leave **YOU** stuck in a rut?

You have to re-word and ultimately *REDESIGN* your resume and job description. An entry level data entry clerk could put "Administrative Assistant" or "Executive Assistant" on her resume. It's all about how you present yourself. Your resume should look like an expensive plate of food from a fancy restaurant. You know! The $150.00 plate with a scoop of garlic mash, one lamb chop, and a string bean on it! Hilarious!

I'll never forget the time I was a college drop out and had no experience. But I needed a job! Sound familiar?

Well, I took matters into my own hands! I created a wonderful resume and started sending it out. It never crossed my mind that I had not done a single one of those jobs on the list. I had a few call backs but couldn't pull through in the interviews so I had to back track a little. I went to a temp agency and submitted my resume. They called the following week and offered me a job! I accepted. Then the recruiter said those dreadful words and almost gave me a heart attack, "Okay, let me check your references and I'll get back to you!"

I'm looking like— man what? I thought I was in. **THEN THE PHONES STARTED RINGING!**

Remember, I didn't have any experience so I put my house phone number, my stepmom's home office number, and my sister's cell down as my reference contact numbers. Man… when I say I was running back and forth through the house changing my voice and shit! My sisters sat on the bed laughing and *REFUSED TO HELP ME!* That's particularly fucked up because Meekie is super good at impersonations. She can do anyone's voice. I could have had a reference from Bill Clinton if she would have helped. And my sister Mae does the best "white lady" voice so yea — they could've been of great help!

Nonetheless, I got the job! I was 19 years old working in a business office at a hospital making $16/hr. **BOOM!**

Better get like me and take that chance! I don't care what you do— there's a way to *SPRUCE IT UP!* You could be the guy that sweeps up the money off the stage at the strip club— STAGE MANAGER at an events venue. You could actually be the stripper— AERIAL FITNESS INSTRUCTOR, CHOREOGRAPHER, CUSTOMER SERVICE REP, etc. It's all about what direction you want to go in your career. You could be a cashier— ACCOUNTS PAYABLE/RECEIVABLE. You could be a janitor-SUPERINTENDENT, CONCIERGE, etc. You get it? Then of course you need to research what all these jobs entail so you can be on point, but you're half way there.

Job Market

First things first, you have to know what jobs are available.

Why do you think most black kids want to be in entertainment (rapper, actor, ball player)? Why do you think some turn to stripping and selling drugs? Because we don't glorify anything else in our community. No one wants to flip burgers. People barely want to be cashiers at a store. No one wants to make just a "decent" living.
WE WANNA HIT IT BIG!

A lot of us watched our mothers catch a bus to and from work to go wipe old people's asses! FOR YEARS! I think about things like that and wonder why black people always pick the "low level" work. I mean, someone has to do it and if that's your passion it could never be "lowly", but for those who don't want that— it's shameful! But why do we end up in these positions? Because we don't know any better.

What does being a garbage man, plumber, and city bus driver have in common? They all make great money and offer benefits. Did you know that with just a high school diploma and passing a civil service test you could get any CITY JOB you apply for? You can do more than work at fast food joints.

Being a mailman is classified as a government job. That means benefits and a pension. I know none of you want to be the police. I agree. Police are suckers. Man they don't even show up when you have a problem. They deliberately wait an hour then sneak by to see if they need to call the coroner. On top of that you can't trust them. They are protecting and serving the interests of the city and it's laws. In 2005, the Supreme Court ruled it's not the police's constitutional duty to protect citizens, only to enforce laws! BUT! Wouldn't you prefer to see more black faces doing **"community policing"** than those over zealous white boys with a "hard on" 'cause they're itchin' to kill a ~~nigga~~????

I'm just saying. A lot of you would rather sit at home and complain all day about how there are no jobs.

THERE ARE MILLIONS OF JOBS! You just have to choose what you want to do and head in that direction.

Think about it this way. I watch all these shows on the travel channel and the home and garden channel. These white people be moving to different countries buying and building homes. It sounds like, "Hi, I'm Matt and I'm a part-time cigar sniffer and my wife Jenna sells umbrella insurance and together we have a budget of $3.8 million." I can't stand it. It's sickening! And don't say- "Oh that's because they're white!" Hell no! It's cause they know what's available.

Go for yours. Stop playing small!

Aptitude Test

Aptitude. Noun. One's natural ability to do something.

Most of you are stuck on what to do because you simply don't know what you can do! What are you capable of? What do you like to do? What's something you would do even if no money was involved? These are all things to think about. Then you need to take an aptitude test or career assessment test and see what field would work best for you. White people are 1000 times ahead of us on this one and let me tell you how.

Before a white kid is born, in "best case" scenarios, a plan was already put together. How many of you are "accidents" and have "accidents"? Well, tell me how the hell in the 9-10 months it took to bring a child into this world you (and your parents) managed not to come up with even a piece of a plan?

That little white baby has a name and father's last name. The parents have already decided he's going to be a firefighter so they've decorated his room with fire engines and Dalmatians and all kinds of fire fighter related items.

Nine times out of ten he'll be a firefighter because that's where he's being guided.

We're more often than not... misguided.

And even if they don't pick the kid's career ahead of time they'll watch the kid to see what (s)he is good at. If the child is a good dancer, then from the onset of walking they'll be in dance classes and going to dance camps. If the kid is a good writer, the parents will find writing workshops and writing camps. They invest in their children. They pay attention to what the kids are good at and they focus on that skill to maximize the fullest potential.

We can't do anything about how our parents messed up. I'm more than sure they didn't know this information either. But you can be the change your family needs.

Conspectus

Relax! A lot of this information is not common knowledge and that's the problem. We can lead exemplary lives.

1. Assess where you are in relation to work. Are you happy? If not, what would make you happy?

2. What are some things you're naturally good at?

3. Do you have a valuable skill? If not, is there a class or workshop you can take to gain a skill?

4. Are you paying attention to what your kids are good at?

5. Are you investing in their interests as a possible career goal and/or way of life?

Apply what you've learned in this chapter and watch things change. Get you a quality resume made and stop sending the same resume around to every job you apply for. Learn to tweak your resume for the position or just seek help on that. It's okay to ask for help.

Acting as if is the same as "praising in the hallway". You know without a doubt that what you want is already yours so you give thanks and live life like it has already happened.

That means you've stepped up and you're playing the role consistently and efficiently. This is a manifestation exercise that always works.

Chapter 5: For Us, By Us!

"Poverty is slavery!" ~ African Proverb

Do you all remember when FUBU hip hop apparel dropped in the 90's? Man everybody was rockin' it and we all loved it because the marketing was genius! "For Us, By Us!" That was a great feeling. It wasn't just a brand, it was a movement! At its peak, in 1998, FUBU grossed over $350 million in worldwide sales. How crazy is that? Yes, it was **black owned**, but it was more about the message! We know it wasn't popular simply because it was black owned, 'cause ya'll don't support black owned businesses today. Such a shame.

As black people we love saying, "We don't have shit! We don't have any black leaders since Martin Luther King, Jr. and Malcolm X were assassinated! We don't have nice things in our community like the other side!" That's because when they rise up— WE DON'T SUPPORT THEM!

Ya'll still talking shit about Colin Kaepernick and boycotting football. Ya'll won't rock certain black owned apparel because it's not " in style"! When we know damn well... *EVERYTHING BLACK PEOPLE DO BECOMES THE STYLE!*

We have to stop making excuses and start supporting each other because herein is where the secret lies.

Think about it.

Asians set up nail shops in our communities. Arabs set up gas stations and clothing stores. White people own the buildings and/or houses we live in and do business in. Yet when you go into their neighborhoods there are no black faces— living there or selling there!

I wonder why that is.

Black Buying Power

What does $1.2 trillion and Black people have in common?

Buying Power.

I'll never forget, around 2012, hearing The Honorable Louis Farrakhan say, *"BOYCOTT BLACK FRIDAY"*! Then he educated black folks of how the system was further enslaving and impoverishing us through **"Holiday Spending"**! He pushed that message for 3 years and in 2015 Time magazine published an article of how Black Friday was down $1 billion dollars. Online shopping was up by 14 percent because some of you just can't follow directions, but even with those who did boycott—
WE MADE A BIG IMPACT!

I'll never forget the "Oscars Blackout" of 2016. For those of you who don't remember, it was the year NO BLACK MOVIES, ACTORS, ACTRESSES, WRITERS, or DIRECTORS were nominated for anything! We decided we would not watch and they had the lowest ratings they'd seen in 8 years! Never forget!

And more recently, I'll never forget how Colin Kaepernick's refusal to stand for the national anthem led to more players protesting which led to him being black balled from the league and called for a full boycott of the NFL! Every week the news was scrambling for answers as to why the ratings had dropped so low. They lost $200 million in viewership in a blink of an eye? Why was the drop progressing every week to the point that ad sales were in jeopardy?

Why?

Black Power!

There's power in our unity! We built this country and we can crumble it. And while most people will get a mental image of us going to war physically— I'm thinking financially. There is no need for a war, only a war in your mind! If they own it all because we buy it all— who really holds the power? I'll give you a hint. If you don't buy from their store— it goes out of business. But what if we refuse to buy from any store in our community that's not black owned? Whoever owns the storefront would be losing money. They would either have to sell the building to one of us or lower the rent and allow us to move a store in. We're that powerful in numbers.

Currently we spend about 3% of our $1.2 trillion with Black owned businesses. Studies show that if we spent just 10% of that $1.2 trillion with Black businesses we would create over 1 million jobs. The jobs many of you claim aren't already out there. Imagine creating that for yourself.

We have to find ways to keep the money IN-HOUSE because you can clearly see where it's going and how their communities are benefiting from it and staying two steps ahead of us.

There's an urban legend about the life span of a dollar in each community by race. The dollar circulates the Asian community for a month before leaving and entering into another community, 20 days in the Jewish community, 17 days in the White community, and a matter of hours in the Black community.

I'm sure there's some truth to it. When we get paid— we spend it. Black women go to nail salons and beauty supply stores owned by Asians. We all go to gas stations owned by Arabs. White people own all the companies we have to pay a bill to. Whether it's your utility company, furniture rental place, or layaway at a store, we don't spend with our own. The Jews own all the banks where our money is held.

We have to shop with the small black owned companies to create more jobs in the community, to ultimately keep more money in-house and build more businesses that create even more jobs. This will build an economic flooring in our community. I'll give you an example.

You could support the black owned grocery store and black owned restaurant. Now more black people have jobs. A husband is the cook at the restaurant and his wife is a cashier at the grocery store. Now they've saved up money to open a barber and beauty shop where they employ other black people. We support their business. We don't know that 2 ambitious young women work at the beauty shop and 2 ambitious young men work at the barbershop. The two young ladies pool their money together and open a beauty supply store. The two barbers open a clothing store. A young black man works at the clothing store and saves up to open up a mechanic shop. Now we have all of this in our neighborhoods run by us and making money for us. What's next? We start to pour into our communities. Clean parks, renovate and maintain schools, etc. And we all know more opportunity means less crime.

Its all connected!

Brand vs. Budget

"...Now the thing is, though, all of us in here getting money — that alone isn't gonna stop this. Alright, dedicating our lives to getting money just to give it right back for someone's brand on our body when we spent centuries praying with brands on our bodies, and now we pray to get paid for brands on our bodies."
~ Jesse Williams (BET Awards, 2016)

That moment was so touching because it accurately describes the foolery that is *"overspending"*. The story goes that as "prisoners of war" we were whipped and branded as if we were property. But if we were wearing the brands of our slave owners why do we now dedicate our lives to making money to "PAY" to wear brand names of those who still own everything? So you went from being on The Hilfiger Plantation wearing their brand on your body to now wearing a shirt with the brand's labels (designer labels as well). These habits are keeping us poor, thus keeping us in bondage. Your favorite celeb gets paid to wear designer labels, but it's costing you money. There's a major difference between the two.

41

When we are born, a lot of our parents immediately buy us brands. We all can recall watching news reports about black people fighting and wrecking stores for the most popular basketball sneaker. That was ingrained in us at a very young age.

But what does Bill Gates wear? The same collar shirt and khaki pants with loafers. He's a billionaire wearing a $50 dollar outfit head to toe. Yet you're a "dollar menunaire" and your outfit cost you upward of $300. Steve Jobs wore the same black turtleneck, blue jeans and sneakers every day like a cartoon character. It's time to deprogram and reprogram, which brings me to my next point.

Budget. Noun. An estimate of income and expenditure for a set period of time. Get familiar with the term. Statistics say the average median annual salary for black people is $35,600, yet we spend an average of $26,000 annually. Something is not right, especially because I know a lot of people who make far less than the median salary, yet spend way more than the spending average.

Time to grab a hold of where we are financially. We need to be honest about how much we are bringing in versus how much is going out. As stated in the previous chapter, you should make at least 3 times your monthly expenses. If you can't buy two in cash that means you really can't afford it. If you can't buy it in cash (instead of using a credit card or borrowing) you can't afford it. Cut back on the spending, especially on fast food, brand names, and businesses that do nothing for our community.

How to set a budget (WikiHow is my favorite):

1. **Set your goal.** Defining a goal makes it easier to stick to your budget, and gives you a way of measuring your success or failure in meeting it. Why are you going on a budget? Maybe you want to start saving for college, or maybe you want to get out of debt. Whatever the case, make sure you set a SMARTER goal (a goal that is Specific,

Measurable, Achievable, Relevant, Time-bound, Evaluated, and Reviewed regularly) to improve your chances at success from the beginning.

2. **Calculate how much money you earn after taxes in a typical month.** Begin by figuring out exactly what you bring home each month— your net income after taxes and other deductions, which includes your paycheck, tips, scholarships, legal entitlements like child support, alimony, government subsidies, and any other money that comes into your wallet or bank account. This is your income.

3. **Calculate your expenses.** Save all of your receipts for a couple weeks, or a month. Knowing your monthly expenditure on groceries or gas, for example, makes the next step much easier. If you want to start writing your budget today but don't have receipts, it is possible, just slightly more difficult.

✦ *Fixed Expenses* are expenses that remain relatively stable from one month to the next. These will include items such as your rent, mortgage payment, car payment, loan payments, utilities, and insurance. A fixed expense that many people overlook is savings. You must pay yourself—in the form of your savings account—before you pay anyone else. This way you can develop a financial "padding" to protect yourself during times of financial hardship.

✦ *Variable Expenses* are items that fluctuate from one month to the next such as the costs associated with dining out, entertainment, clothing, groceries, personal care products, and vacations. This will be the first place to make cutbacks if you are spending beyond your means.

4.   **Divide your budget into basic categories.** For example: "Housing," "Food," "Auto," "Entertainment," "Savings," "Clothing," "Medical," and "Miscellaneous." You could also organize your expenses into needs - such as your loan and electricity - and wants - such as clothing and entertainment.

5.   **List all your spending for each category.** Let's take "Auto" as an example, and say that each month you have a car payment of $300 and a $100 insurance bill. In addition, every month you spend an average of $250 on fuel, $50 on maintenance, and $10 on taxes and fees, such as registration. So, in the "Auto" category, your total budget for the month would need to be at least $710 per month. If, for some reason, you don't know the exact amounts you spend in a category, make good estimates. The more accurate you are, the more likely you are to keep to your budget plan.

6.   **Add up all your spending by categories.** This should show your total monthly spending, or how much money you take out of your wallet or bank account each month. Compare it to your income.

7.   **Decide on a method to keep track of your budget.** You can use a good old-fashioned ledger book, available from a general shopping center for about $5. However, many people prefer to use computer programs like Quicken, Microsoft Money, or Excel. **There's an app for that!**

8.   **Set up your ledger.** If you chose to get the ledger book, leave the first five odd pages blank, we'll come back to them later. Divide the rest of the ledger into as many sections as you have main categories. Put each main category on the first page of each section. This will give you room for lots of entries in each category. Multiple transaction

categories, like "Food," are going to need lots of pages.

9.   **Show a "deposit" in each category at the start of each period, then show all the expenditures from that category throughout the period.** So, for "Auto" you would start off with $710 for the month, then show several expenditures for "fuel", one expenditure for "car payment", and maybe one expenditure for "insurance" (depending on whether you pay for insurance monthly).

10. **Make adjustments.** In order to devise a balanced budget and meet your goal, your income must be greater than or equal to your expenses. To find out if your budget is balanced, you need to subtract your fixed and variable expenses from your income.

+   *The Balanced Budget.* If your income is the same as your expenses, or, better yet, greater than your expenses, you have devised a fully functioning working budget. Though it may be tempting to spend whatever "extra" funds you have, your next step ought to be to make sure that you put your leftover funds to work for you. There is no such thing as "money to spare," especially if you have debt or unrealized savings goals. Instead of adding your surplus to the "Fun" budget, always use it pay down your debt and add to your savings.

+   *The Unbalanced Budget.* If you are spending more than you earn or receive, you have some serious work to do to balance your budget. Begin by examining and adjusting your variable expenses. You will need to scale back on this spending first by cutting back on luxury expenses, like restaurants, entertainment, and other non-necessities (e.g., latest trend products). If your budget is still out of whack, try cutting back on fixed expenses too. Perhaps you can rent a room or take on a roommate to share your bills. Or, maybe, you need to opt for a cheaper or more fuel-efficient car. Conversely, you can also try to increase your income by taking on part-time labor, working overtime (if it is available), switching jobs, or starting a home-based business.

> *Evaluate* continually. Your financial situation will change; therefore, it is necessary to make alterations to your budget from time to time. If you pay off a debt, get a raise, or make some other life change, rework your budget using your new information. And remember, debt repayment, savings, and financial security must always be your number one priorities.[9]

Money Mindset vs. Poverty Mindset

According to SelfGrowth.com, a poverty mentality is a mindset about money that develops over time - it is a "poor me" attitude that stems from a deep-seated belief that there is never enough. Persistent thoughts and comments such as "I can't afford this…" and "I'll never have enough money to have that…" may turn out to be a self-fulfilling prophecy.[10]

I whole-heartedly believe poverty starts in the mind. Don't crucify me like we did that Black man, Ben Carson the neurosurgeon, that Donald Trump put in charge of HUD Housing. I personally would be pissed as hell if I'd built an empire for myself as a leading neurosurgeon, but because I'm black I'm only seen as being fit to overlook Section 8 housing for the poor. Shows how much they think about you man. But I digress.

Ben Carson said, "People with the "right mind set" can have everything taken away from them, and they'll pull themselves up. You take somebody with the wrong mind-set, you can give them everything in the world (and) they'll work their way right back down to the bottom."[11]

That, my friends, is so true. There's an old saying, "We can take all the money in the world and divide it up evenly amongst everyone and within 5 years the rich will be rich again and the poor will be destitute."

So maybe it's not all in the mind. Yes! There are socio-economic issues that exist due to systemic racism. There are many. Like, less job opportunities in "low income" areas, and the very low wages from the jobs that are available. But how many of these people actually apply for higher paying jobs? But if the higher paying jobs are across town and I can't afford a car, I'm still at a disadvantage on public transportation. But how many of these people actually finished high school so they could qualify? How many have a criminal record? Oh it gets deep and it's all connected. But right now I want to talk about what we can fix.

Well, first we have to unlearn what we were taught! If you're Black and you know it raise your hand. So that means everybody with their hand raised has been told by their mother and/or grandmother- *"Money don't grow on trees"!* That's where it all started. As Black people, we are taught you have to work hard for money. Money's not easy to come by. You have to be super smart to make a lot of money. You have to already have a leg up. All of that is a lie! A wealthy mindset believes- ***"I am abundant in every way." "Money flows easy to me." "I am enough."*** And one way to create that is by not living above your means.

I will never understand how we as Black People have the highest rate of poverty in the country, but spend more than all other races combined. We are consumers. But I think I know why.

Dr. Umar Johnson was on "The Breakfast Club" with *Charlamagne The God, Angela Yee, and DJ Envy*. He said black people overspend because it creates an *"illusion of freedom"*. The Constitution said it's one's unalienable rights to life, liberty, and the pursuit of happiness; but we found out later they were speaking of "white men with property", only. So some associate "white privilege" with what it means to be "free". White people have nice homes in the suburbs with a family vehicle and a fun vehicle. So

47

in return Black people will live in debt and risk losing everything for the sake of the "illusion".

Many feel that if we can have what they have and do what they do— we're good! But one thing we don't consider is how they do it versus how we do it. WE go out of our way to get these car loans with these high ass interest rates. We sit down to buy a $14,000 and by the time we're done paying it off, we've paid upward of $20,000. Meanwhile, the white guy probably took $10k-$12k and went to the dealership and bought it cash, OR he leased it. So the same $425.69 you're paying per month for 5 years for a Ford Fusion, they're paying maybe $330 per month for that one year on a luxury vehicle and then they'll trade it in and get the newer version. So at the end of the day— YOU STILL AREN'T FREE!

Debt, just like poverty, IS **SLAVERY**! Yes! There are millions of white slaves due to debt. But there are millions that are **FINANCIALLY FREE!** I mean 720+ credit score (FICO), make six figures or close to it, have a savings account and assets. So they can afford it. Can you? And if you can't, don't trip. This book is building the mindset that will get you there.

I was once in debt. I used to get a tax time car every year. My credit score was in the 400's. I was fucked up. *BUT I WAS LIVING LAVISH!* Baby they couldn't tell me nothing! We have got to break that mindset as a unit. I broke it and was debt free just 2 years later! It can happen! Most of us don't have a problem with making money. It's keeping it we struggle with.

We need to stop biting off more than we can chew. If you've been upside down on bills your whole life, started from childhood like I did, it's time to stop that shit! Stop making more bills for yourself. If you can't afford that high ass cable, you need Netflix, Hulu, and/or Amazon Fire TV stick. Stop dropping $300 every time you go to the mall. You DO NOT need a new outfit for every occasion! You're watching too much TV.

The wealthy do not struggle to flaunt their wealth.

Ever heard of "Keeping Up With The Joneses"? That's not just something we say in the hood. ***Keeping up with the Joneses*** is an idiom in many parts of the English-speaking world referring to the comparison to one's neighbor as a benchmark for social class or the accumulation of material goods. To fail to "**keep up with the Joneses**" is perceived as demonstrating socio-economic or cultural inferiority.[12] So honey, when your credit is bad and your shit is in collections all the time, you are failing to keep up with *The Joneses*. But if you pay attention, by the end of the book you *The Joneses* will be keeping up with you.

Conspectus

I want to challenge you right now.

For the next 21 days, I challenge you (and your family) to stop excess spending by doing the following:

1. Stop going out to the club every weekend and when you do go, don't spend more than your budget says you can comfortably. Set the amount before the night starts.

2. Buy groceries and cook instead of buying fast food. Cook enough to bring lunch to work in order to avoid wasting money.

3. Dress for less. Find a cheaper place to shop that still looks nice. All those side stores have a nice knock off version of whatever you're looking at in the department stores.

4. Get it out of your head that you have something to prove.

5. Make sure you make a budget so you can know where you are financially and where you can trim some fat.

6. Stop associating wealth with material things and start seeing money as a tool. I always say *"Black people get money and buy cars and clothes. White people get money and buy politicians."* What I mean by that is, power can get you things money can't buy.

7. For the next 21 days, save whatever money you have and/or get paid that is not going toward bills this month.

Thank me later.

Chapter 6: The 700 Club

"Borrowing is like a wedding, repaying is like mourning..." ~Swahili Proverb

You ever loaned money to someone and not only were they taking too long to pay you back, but you saw them around town balling out and living their best lives? Well, that's how creditors feel when you don't pay back what you owe. The best way not to get into those type of situations is to not borrow in the first place. But how can you not? In America, credit is advertised all around you. I walked into a grocery store and was offered a credit card. Excessive.

But what is credit really saying? Buy now, **PAY LATER** is what it's saying. But where most people go wrong is they look at it as EXTRA MONEY. So basically it's the same as if your friend gives you a pre-paid debit card with a $300 balance on it to borrow and you use it, but never pay them back. That's disloyal. At that point the creditors feel like you can't be trusted to repay your debts so not only will they not work with you again, but they're also going to put your info in a database to let all the other potential creditors know you don't pay people back! Now that I think about it— we need that system amongst friends and family. Haha!

But that's exactly how credit works. There are three major credit bureaus- Equifax, Experian, and Transunion. A credit bureau is a company that gathers and stores various types of information about you and your financial accounts and history. They draw on this information to create your credit reports and credit scores (which ranges from 300-850). This helps other creditors make lending decisions.[13] How do I know that? Research! I got it from CreditKarma.com which is the simplest site when you first start learning about credit and finances. Write that down if you haven't heard of it.

Credit is such a big deal nowadays, even jobs are looking at your credit to determine your qualifications as an employee. So you must be knowledgeable of it. But even more important is learning how to use it properly. Once you get the hang of it, you too can get in *"The 700 Club"*. It's more exclusive than the top Hollywood parties. Let's jump right in.

Credit Repair

I'll never forget my first credit card! I was super excited. It was a $500 credit card from Bank of America. After some time they raised the limit to $1000. Still to this day I can't tell you what I was doing right or wrong on that card. I don't know. But they cut that card off abruptly. I paid it off a year later and they didn't offer me another card from 2007 to 2015! I applied several times and they weren't trying to hear it. But I was on and off again with staying on track financially so they did me a favor. Then I decided I had to get serious about my credit cause I wanted to be in a position to never be broke again and to never be turned down for anything again. So I researched ways to repair my credit on my own.

First thing I did was dispute everything that was older than 7 years old on my credit. That instantly gave me a boost! So many of us don't know anything about credit so we don't know most "charge-offs" or negative items on your credit report are supposed to be removed in 7 years according to the **Fair Credit Reporting Act**. Creditors can no longer hold it against you. There were also some charges still showing as outstanding that had been paid. You have to make sure you pay attention to it cause a lot of us really have a good credit score, but just have to blow some of the dust off.

One thing that will kill your credit though is not paying your student loans. That shit hits hard AND what the student loan companies do is KEEP CLOSING ACCOUNTS AND OPENING OTHERS. That hurts your score so much because it looks like you keep taking out loans and not paying them back. It's all a game.

But back to the story.

Through my research I learned a lot of people repair their credit by getting secured credit cards. A secured card requires a cash collateral deposit that becomes the credit line for that account.[14] For example, if you put $500 in the account, you can charge up to $500. So I applied to get one from Capital One. Instead they sent me a card with a $300 limit. I was extra careful this time. I only spent 30% or under on my card and always paid more than the monthly minimum. Most of the time I paid the whole thing off. Before I knew it, my limit was up to $3000! The limit on that one card is almost $10K and it was $300 under 5 years ago! The crazy part is it would be higher if I stayed on track and didn't waver as much as I did. You have to work at it continuously.

During that time, I was careful not to put anything else on my credit. For a while I just bought everything in cash. If I couldn't buy it without credit I didn't need it. Credit is anything you can "buy now and pay later" on, from financing a car to putting furniture in your name. Setting up those cell phones with major networks goes on your credit as well. You have to pay attention to those things. With doing just these few things AND making payment plans on small amounts I could pay off quickly, I raised my credit score by almost 300 points in 2 years! You just have to do the work.

Secured Loan

I mentioned the secured credit card where you can put the money down to act as the line of credit. The same can be done with a loan. Quite a few banks and most credit unions offer secured loans. In fact, my sister used it to raise her credit. She opened an account with a small bank and deposited $1200 to borrow against and paid it off over time. You don't have to start that high. Just a few hundred will do. So this is how it works. You walk in a bank, tell them you want to open an account and take out a secured loan (or do so with your current account). You'll put the money in your account and sign "loan" paperwork to "borrow against your own money". So they'll turn around and give you their $1200 and hold yours until their's is paid back. I actually took one out for my first business. The best part about it is you get your money back when you pay it off AND it makes you eligible for more loans AND higher lines of credit. So it's just another way to beat the system.

Inherited Credit

This is the one I just found out about within the past few years. It's a seasoned trade line and basically what you can do is **"Piggyback"** off someone else's credit. Let's say I'm your sister, mom, cousin, whomever— I'm in the "The 700 Club" meaning my FICO score is 700 or more. Most people shoot for a 720! That's like prime rib to creditors. They eat it up. So my credit is good, but you on the other hand, have "bad credit". What I can do is, add you as an **AUTHORIZED USER** on one of my credit cards (in good standing with a high limit) and that will give you an immediate boost in score.

Another way to take advantage of this is something Black people do all the time, but do it horribly wrong- PUT SHIT IN YOUR KIDS' NAMES! Black people have been doing this since the beginning of time- and *"messin them churn names up"*! My sister still clowns me to this day saying our mama put a Gateway desktop computer in my name when I was 12 years old! She saw the bill for it. Or we could talk about the time I was 18 or 19 and my mom had a Comcast bill in my name and ran it up to over $800! I still have no clue how the bill got that high! Like what were ya'll doing? Ordering movies all day? Why would the cable company allow it to get that high? Shit! You know how they do, probably kept adding on fees cause my ghetto family didn't return their illegal cable box. That's horrible! And I got mad and said I'm not paying it! I'll make a police report on my mama before I pay that damn bill because I'm grown now and it's time to show people you can't just play with my time, my money, my name, my social, or any of that.

Now let me tell you how WHITE FOLKS do this shit. Let's say, David and Allison have a kid. They don't have the best credit, but they're working on it, especially now since they've started a family. They want to be responsible. So David and Allison do some research on ways to make money for the kid, through the kid. They find out Gerber Life Insurance has a package option that pays for your kid to go to college, so they pick that up. Then they come across some financially savvy friends who tell them to open up a credit card in the kid's name. But keep the card in good standing. They use that credit to help clean up their's. Now they have 3 names with good credit. Once the kid is around 16 it's already set, but they take it a step further. They register a business in the kid's name and start making payments to the kid through the "name of the company" (whether it's a running business or just another "Name"). Once that kid turns 18 he'll be so far ahead of the game he'll be speaking in numbers. And guess what— NOW they can take out a line of credit against the business name! That's 4 NAMES WITH **LINES OF CREDIT IN GOOD STANDING!** That's why the economic ratios are as they are today! They know the secrets and how to implement them.

Insurance

Insurance. I know most of you have never heard of that word other than this book. I know that because every time a black person dies *"A Fish Fry Gets It's Wings"*. Meanwhile, when a white person dies— a show on the ID channel gets a new episode, 'cause in most cases somebody got killed for the insurance money. Hilarious! Yes... that was stereotypical, but I had to. Haha! But all jokes aside— most of them are millionaires because someone died and left them insurance money– AND THEIR FAMILIES DID THE RIGHT THINGS WITH THE MONEY! Black folks still out here thinking they can get rich and never have to work again! That's a lie! How do you stay rich if you don't make the money work for you? You don't! You go broke! I'm tired of my people not handling their funds correctly. Some never get off the ground and most that hit it big- GO BROKE!

Now back to the point.

My fiancé tries to explain the importance of insurance to me all the time and I'm just like, "Well I'm young so I'm not going to die." "I want to be cremated anyway because it's just the body, I'm not in it anymore." Then he explained to me how insurance could be an asset, meaning it could make money for me. Who doesn't want to make more money? But no matter how many times he explained it to me- I just wasn't getting it. So what did I do? I RESEARCHED IT! Now I'm going to share my findings and understanding of it. You take what you can from it and RESEARCH for a further understanding.

"Deciding whether to purchase whole life or term life insurance is a personal decision that should be based on the financial needs of your beneficiaries as well as your financial goals. Life insurance can be a very flexible and powerful financial vehicle that can meet multiple financial objectives, from providing financial security to building financial assets and leaving a legacy." [15]

With the first 2 sentences I knew I was on the right track because I'm one of the very few people I know that talk about "leaving a legacy". Most people I know want to make sure they can live good and take care of their kids, but on the other side of the tracks white folks are *preparing for GENERATIONS TO COME*. That's why they have far more, they need it. It's a mindset. Next they broke it down into sections:

Features of Term Life Insurance

- *Provides death benefits only*
- *Pays benefits only if you die while the term of the policy is in effect*
- *Easiest and most affordable life insurance to buy*
- *Purchased for a specific time period, such as 5, 10, 15, or 30 years, known as a "term"*
- *Becomes more expensive as you age, especially after age 50*
- *The term must be renewed if you want coverage to be extended beyond the term length*
- *Can be used as temporary additional coverage with a permanent life insurance policy*
- *Can be converted to whole life insurance*

56

Features of Whole Wife Insurance:

- *Covers you for life*
- *Provides death benefits as well as a cash value accumulation that builds during the life of the policy*
- *You typically must qualify with a health examination*
- *Can be purchased without a medical exam, but at a higher cost*
- *Takes 12 to 15 years to build u decent cash value*
- *Can be a good choice for estate planning*
- *Cash value is based on how much the return on investment is worth*
- ***A portion of the cash value can be withdrawn or borrowed during the life of the policy.***
- *Initially has more expensive premiums than term life insurance, but can potentially save you money over the life of the policy if in force for a considerable number of years*

So I take it many people choose "Term Life" instead of "Whole Life" because they are thinking about covering final costs and their children being taken care of until they can fend for themselves. It's cheaper as well. Sounds good to me. As long as you have something set up you are fine, but do your research.

BUT I MUST POINT OUT... WHITE FOLKS GOT WHOLE LIFE INSURANCE! And here is why.

Look at the features. What word stands out? Cash. Look at the second to last bullet point. A portion of the cash value can be withdrawn or borrowed during the life of the policy! Aha! That's how many of them send their kids to college. That's also another source of money to invest in a rental property or to act as a small business loan! You sleep!

My fiancé even borrowed from a policy his dad set up for him. He had to pay it back. Don't forget that part black people. You have to pay back what you owe!

Conspectus

I know how you're feeling. You feel like you just hit the next level of the game! You have! And I know many of you are feeling like you're so behind. No honey, you're right on time. You've been seeking a new way of doing things. You didn't choose this book. This book chose you. Am I wrong? For a while you've been feeling like you need to get your shit together and don't know which way to turn. Or you may feel like our people as a whole need to get on the same page. I felt the same way- FOR A WHILE! So I decided to write this book.

I cleaned up my credit and had money saved in a matter of 2 years. You can too! It's about making a sacrifice. What will you sacrifice now so that you can live the life of your dreams later?

- Are you willing to sacrifice your time? Meaning, can you work your regular 8 hour shift and go home and still carve out an hour or two to work on your goals?

- Are you willing to sacrifice your money by purchasing courses and other learning materials?

- Are you willing to sacrifice your instant gratification for consistent hard work?

- Are you willing to cut back on your spending, get a roommate or live with your family members? Are you willing to relocate?

What are you willing to sacrifice for the goals you wish to achieve?

Don't let pride and people seeing you starting at the bottom keep you from starting on the journey you've been dreaming about.

When it comes to credit... guard your's. It's your reputation with businesses. What do you want them to say about you? Credit is easy to borrow, but very hard to pay back because interest accrues daily. Credit cards, student loans and evictions are not the only charges that can affect your credit score.

Don't be out here co-signing for anyone. That's on both of your credit reports. Any missed payments will affect your credit as well. If your car gets repossessed that's a hard hit to your credit. Unpaid medical bills and utilities all have an effect on your credit score. Remember that.

Your credit is your reputation. Make sure you're always in good standing. Bad credit is not a death sentence, but it sure as hell can be on life support and still capable of a full recovery.

Get started on that.

Chapter 7: Follow Success

"If you close your eyes to facts, you will learn through accidents..." ~ African Proverb

Success leaves clues.

You like that don't you?

I know you do because I remember how I felt when I first heard it. It makes all the sense in the world. When you look at successful people you notice one thing they all have in common- *THEY FOLLOW SUCCESS*. What does that mean? They all have someone who inspired them, whom they have modeled themselves after. A lot of entertainers say they used to watch Michael Jackson and wanted to be like him. They studied his music and his moves. One of those entertainers is Beyonce. See where I'm going with this?

If you don't want a black man to know something— PUT IT IN A BOOK.

Have you ever heard that saying before? When's the last time you read a book? A news article? A stop sign? Anything other than an Instagram meme?

Successful people read. A lot. Useful information— not gossip.

The Huffington Post interviewed Warren Buffet in 2016 and asked about his keys to success:

He pointed to a stack of nearby books and said, *"Read 500 pages like this every day. That's how knowledge works. It builds up, like compound interest. All of you can do it, but I guarantee not many of you will do it."*

Bill Gates reads about 50 books per year, which breaks down to 1 per week.
Mark Cuban reads more than 3 hours every day.
Elon Musk is an avid reader and when asked how he learned to build rockets, he said, *"I read books"*.
Mark Zuckerberg read a book every 2 weeks in 2015.
Oprah Winfrey selects one of her favorite books every month for her Book Club members to read and discuss.[16]

Now don't think you can just read blog pages all day and get ahead. Don't think you can read *"Zane's Sex Chronicles"* and get ahead unless you're a sex therapist or counselor of some sort. It's not just that they are reading. It's what they're reading. Pick a person who you admire and would like to model your life after. Google them. Read their life story. Find out if they've written a book. Then google what books they recommend reading. Jay-Z and Oprah are my two picks. I've read their stories. I've read a few books that they've read. The Celestine Prophecy is one that Jay-Z recommended and when I read it, not only did it open me up deeper to some things I'd already been studying for myself, but it also made me look at him completely different. But most of all, I felt great because I felt it meant I was on the right track. Out of the 6 pieces that influenced him I've read 5 of them. Which reminds me… I need to re-read his book, *Decoded.*

I named 7 people who are amazingly successful and well read. Five of them were white. Warren Buffet, billionaire business investor. Bill Gates, billionaire owner of Microsoft. Mark Cuban, billionaire owner of the Dallas Mavericks. Elon Musk, billionaire Tesla co-founder. Mark Zuckerberg, billionaire founder of Facebook.

This is not a coincidence my friends. There must be something to it. Some of the keys are hiding in plain sight. Some are in books.

Like Father, Like Son

Have you ever heard of a book called *"Rich Dad, Poor Dad"*? Written by Robert Kiyosaki, it talks about how he developed his unique economic perspective. He watched his dad and his friend's dad and how they handled their finances. His father was well educated, but poor. His friend's dad was a multi-millionaire who dropped out of school in the 8th grade. Imagine that. It's worth a read, but I want to point our a few key excerpts from the book.

"My two dads had opposing attitudes in thought. One dad thought that the rich should pay more in taxes to take care of those less fortunate. The other said, "Taxes punish those who produce and reward those who don't produce."

One dad recommended, "Study hard so you can find a good company to work for." The other recommended, "Study hard so you can find a good company to buy"… One dad said, "The reason I'm not rich is because I have you kids." The other said, "The reason I must be rich is because I have you kids."

One encouraged talking about money and business at the dinner table. The other forbade the subject of money to be discussed over a meal. One said, "When it comes to money, play it safe, don't take risks." The other said, "Learn to manage risk."

Both dads paid their bills on time, yet one paid his bills first and the other paid himself first…One dad struggled to save a few dollars. The other simply created investments… One dad taught me how to write an impressive résumé so I could find a good job. The other taught me how to write strong business and financial plans so I could create jobs.

Being a product of two strong dads allowed me the luxury of observing the effects different thoughts have on one's life. I noticed that people really do shape their life through the thoughts."[17]

I had to give you those excerpts for you to see that it's important for us to learn this information to pass on to our kids. Kiyosaki was lucky enough to have access to a third party so that he could get this information. This is what we don't have. It starts at home. How many black parents do you think understand what this book is trying to teach? Many have never even heard of it. Sometimes it's not that we don't want the information, we just don't know it's out there. We don't know what questions to ask. But hopefully this opens your mind.

Another reason I chose to use Robert Kiyosaki's "Rich Dad, Poor Dad" as an example is because he's Asian. Every ethnicity, culture, community, etc., has its own set of rules that it lives by. From my conversations with Asians I can tell they are all about building through group economics. A friend of mine said in their family when you borrow money you have to pay it back. If you have not paid it back in a timely fashion and someone else is in need, they are sent to you and you must help them or you'll suffer severe consequences. I also heard they'll pool (let's say) $100,000 together for someone to start a business. The business operates and they all receive their investments back so they can go help the next person. Now that you have a business you can also invest and get a return. See how that works? Everybody eats and it keeps the community growing.

I don't want to be stereotypical because not all Asian families are the same (obviously because Kiyosaki's family wasn't like this and I didn't specify which Asian culture) just like not all black families are the same. But think about it this way. Asians are the fastest growing race group in the U.S. That's true in both population and wealth. They have the lowest voter turnout. Yet, they have their own communities (schools, businesses, etc.) and buy within their own. They don't rely on the government for much of anything.

Follow success.

College vs. Trade

Everyone thinks you have to go to school to be educated. Not true. In fact, a person that is only educated at school is "uneducated" when it comes to real life. People with college degrees sometimes act snooty like they're better. I have a degree so I know that isn't true. All a degree means is that you can complete something. That's why I take pride in having a degree. I felt like it was one of the first things I'd ever fully completed in my life. I would usually leave unfinished business and this was the start of something amazing for me personally. Other than that…

I WANT MY MONEY BACK!

Everyone that knows me knows I loathe formal education. I'm so against it. Why? Because I've learned so much outside of school that I now realize most of what I learned in school was useless. We know I have a degree which means I finished college. So I think I have enough experience with going to school that I can carefully deduce that school is a waste. For me, I didn't find anything useful after 8th grade. Now don't you all go dropping out at once. I would never recommend that.

School needs to be revamped and traditional college needs to be done away with. Let me explain.

"What did you learn in high school that you still use today?" All of you probably need some time to think. And once you finally come up with something it will be maybe 1 or 2 things if you're lucky. The rest of it you didn't retain well enough even if you needed to use it again. That's ridiculous. But look at it my way.

In high school you have the athletes, male and female who go on to play in the league or become coaches. You have the cheerleaders and dance team members who go on to college and do the same. Some go to the league as well. Some become background dancers and go on tour with major artists. If you were a part of the student government you probably have a social work job now. If you were in drama club or band you probably went on to become an entertainer.

Do you see where I'm going with this? Career assessment should be more of the focus- NOT TRIGONOMETRY! I haven't seen a damn scientific calculator since I left school! That's $60 down the drain. Sure they're under $20 these days, but back then that put a strain on my low income housing pockets. And it's truly horrible that school puts that type of pressure on families.

Moving right along. You don't really learn anything that comes from the core curriculum side after 8th grade. It's more of the extra curricular activities and electives that we actually want. What high school needs to do is administer an assessment test. Then build a core curriculum around interests.

There are six career categories:

- **Realistic (Do'er)-** Prefers physical activities that require skill, strength, and coordination. Traits include genuine, stable, conforming, and practical. Example professions include architect, farmer, and engineer.

- **Investigative (Thinker)**- Prefers working with theory and information, thinking, organizing, and understanding. Traits include: analytical, curious, and independent. Example professions include lawyer, mathematician, and professor.

- **Artistic (Creator)**- Prefers creative, original, and unsystematic activities that allow creative expression. Traits include: imaginative, disorderly, idealistic, emotional, and impractical. Example professions include: artist, musician, and writer.

- **Social (Helper)**- Prefers activities that involve helping, healing, or developing others. Traits include cooperative, friendly, sociable, and understanding. Example professions include counselor, doctor, and teacher.

- **Enterprising (Persuader)**- Prefers competitive environments, leadership, influence, selling, and status. Traits include ambitious, domineering, energetic, and self-confident. Example professions include Management, Marketing, and Sales Person.

- **Conventional (Organizer)**- Prefers precise, rule-regulated, orderly, and unambiguous activities. Traits include conforming, efficient, practical, unimaginative, and inflexible. Example professions include accountant, clerk and editor.[18]

There could be six different options of core curriculum tailored to the student that fits the profile. It would be much more helpful and more of a guide. Currently it's not teaching the children how to maximize and capitalize on their potential. It's only training them to sit 8 hours in a workplace and follow policy and procedure. The same handbook they get at high school came in your packet when you started your job. It's all a game.

My proposed educational system would create an environment where we don't have people enrolling in a 4 year college for a degree of GENERAL STUDIES and bullshit around for 2 years until they decide- *"I'll just get a degree in Early Childhood Education."* Nothing wrong with that, but you could have saved your money.

That's why I'm an advocate for trade school. **Solid Occupational Outlook.** Learn a viable skill and keep it moving. You don't have to sit in college the first 2 years going over what you learned in high school. That's a waste of time considering most of us barely wanted to do the shit in high school. Of course they would never really push this because college makes so much money off your indecisiveness about your life.

But this is what you can do. Instead of a 4 year university you could choose a program specifically for your goals. For example, my sister-in-law went back to college for her Master's Degree so she could be "Head of Human Resources" at her job. WTF? I'm sorry but that sounds like something you could take a few classes on the weekend and get certified to do. But some of these companies require it. I have a Bachelor's in Mass Communications. I'm a journalist. Not one time has anyone asked to see my degree or even inquired of whether I have one or not. The worst part is that lately I've been hearing people say- *"Oh no! Nowadays a Bachelor's degree is like a high school diploma."* Imagine what's running through my head as I'm hearing people say they agree with this.

I'm sitting there thinking, " I know you a got damn lie!" Don't you know how much money people paid for those degrees? I didn't really have to pay for much of anything because I had the **HOPE Scholarship,** but I transferred to different colleges so many times and even went to private ones which are more expensive so I picked up a student loan or two. Nothing big. BUT *I KNOW PEOPLE WITH $60,000-$100,000 IN STUDENT LOAN DEBT!* Please use scholarships to pay for college if you want to go. Otherwise, it's just not worth it. Think about it… The idea is for you to get the degree and go into your field and make that type of money PER YEAR so that you can pay the loan back. But how many actually do so? For the doctors and engineers this is a breeze, if they're working. For the rest of us who actually went on to work in our field, it'll still take a while. But what about those who don't go on to work in their fields? What about them you ask? Well, what about when they get out here in the real world and they've been in college 5-6 years (most take that long to complete a 4 year degree) and finally graduate only to find out *THE JOB THEY WANT REQUIRES 2+ YEARS OF WORK EXPERIENCE* so you still have to start at an ENTRY LEVEL POSITION. Yea, I'd be pissed too. Some people are facing the sad reality that they paid $100K for a college degree just to land a $40K/year job. There are so many ways this could go for you. So it's up to you to decide what's best. Manage the risk.

Here are a few of the top trade school jobs:
- Elevator Installer/Repairer
- Radiation Therapist
- Geological and Petroleum Technician
- Web Developer
- Dental Hygienist
- Diagnostic Medical Sonographer
- Respiratory Therapist
- Electrician

The training required is anywhere from 6 months to 2 years and they all pay $50,000 or more! It's your life. But I say go for the- *SOLID OCCUPATIONAL OUTLOOK.* You can live your best life without all the added stress. It was hell trying to figure out how to work and go to college all those years. With these options you get on-the-job training while completing the program.

Fail Forward

Right now in the *Social Media Era*, we can see everyone's life. Or so we think. It's so easy to get caught up in the glitz and glamour of pictures. One thing I want to encourage you to do is *"Follow Success"*, but do not *"Imitate"* or *"Copy Cat"*. The reason I'm telling you this is because we can get so caught up in watching people win and enjoying their success that we forget they actually went through a lot behind the scenes. We only see the "highlight reel". So subsequently, you think you're going to have a linear path to success. And what happens when you find out the road to success is paved with potholes and obstacles, wrong turns and four way stops? You get discouraged and get off track. You get depressed. You feel like a loser. That's exactly why you need this information.

Every successful person has a treasure chest full of losses. Oh the stories we could tell of trial and triumph.

I used to be one of those people, so afraid of making a mistake. Seriously! But what I didn't realize is *"Mistakes Are How We Learn"!* Michael Jordan is considered the best basketball player in history. He has six championship rings. Does that mean he played 6 games in his career? Does that mean only the six games he won for the rings actually matter? He played 1,072 regular season games in his 15 seasons in the NBA. Did he win every one? No! He played 15 seasons and won 6 rings. That means he didn't win a championship for 9 other seasons. That means he lost more than he won! But do the losses matter? Do we ever talk about his losses? Aha! No one will remember the times you tripped. They'll only remember the times you won! So don't be afraid or ashamed to struggle. You must keep moving forward.

Let me tell you one of the top reason people fail- THEY QUIT! This is true, especially in this day-in-age with the **"Instant Gratification"** and this unrealistic sense of entitlement. This is the age of the quitter. That's crazy when you think about how so many millennials have struck rich off the smallest things— simple things like funny social media videos. You could simply have a large following on Instagram and people will pay you to promote their product. It seems pretty simple to me. The problem comes in where EVERYONE tries to use the same blueprint. It's not that everyone can't win. It's just that you have to win in your own way. Maybe one person makes funny videos and you're not funny, but you can do hair and make up. Make style tutorials. Maybe your homeboy plays sports and he's going to the league, but you are fat and never played sports. Well, what can you do? Can you be a body guard for him or the other players? Can you cook and become a chef to the stars? If you can't even think that far because you're so caught up in wanting to be in the league — STOP IT! Moments like this are where winners are made. You still want to be in the league? The guys who set up the water and makes sure the balls are inflated make like $50,000 per season. Yes. The "water boy" makes more than you. Ain't that some shit? Each one of those organizations have front office jobs as well. That means you can still be in the league without being a player.

THIS IS HOW SUCCESSFUL PEOPLE THINK!

There are no wrong turns. There are only paths you didn't know you had to take. When things are bad and shit just isn't going your way, think of it as your GPS saying *"REROUTING"*! And we all know how many times that bitch can re-route. So hang in there. Mistakes mean you're on the right path. Don't keep making the same ones. There are messages hidden in each new adventure. Learn from them. Good Luck!

Conspectus

Your life, your love, your health, your finances and your success is YOUR RESPONSIBILITY! We don't grow up knowing any of this. Most of us aren't even born to parents who can teach us this. That's what this chapter is about. I was just like you. I didn't know anything and thought I knew EVERYTHING! It really took for me to fall down and scrape up my knees, elbows, and the side of my face to finally get it.

School is not for everyone, but learning is. We all learn differently. You have to do some self discovery and figure out what works best for you. You can learn something from everyone, even bums on the street. If you sat down and listened to some of their stories you would become very open minded about life and the strengths and vulnerabilities of the people who are living life— that's all of us.

I'm the offspring of what a lot of you and your parents would call, the scum of the earth.

My parents were street legends! Today they are a former drug addict and a convicted murderer that's serving a life sentence. But I'm a college graduate and a business owner.

Hell, I wrote this book!

No excuses. I wanted something different so I went got it.

Success leaves clues. Follow them.

Excuses are easy to make. Allowing the self-sabotaging thoughts to take over causing you not to act is easy. Being fearful and doubtful of your capabilities is easy and quite normal. Going for what you want and making that shit happen is hard. It's very hard.

No one said it would be easy, we only said it would be worth it.

For the people who come from nothing I always give this piece of advice.

If you're from the bottom, there's no where to go, but up. If you're from the bottom, you might as well go for it. Go for your dreams full force. Only two things can happen. You can try and fail and everyone still loves you because they didn't expect you to make it that far...

Oh... but if you **WIN**....

Chapter 8:
Know Your Worth, Then Add Tax

*"If you think you're too small to make a
difference, you've obviously never spent the night
with a mosquito." ~ African Proverb*

"You don't get what you deserve; you get what you
negotiate!"

That valuable information did not come from an Ivy
League grad or a business man. It came from Chrissy
Lampkin on Love and Hip Hop New York. See. I told you-
you can learn something from anyone, anywhere.

I have stories about the times I could have GOTTEN IT
ALL, but I only got a little bit because I didn't play my
cards right.

Here's a little story my fiancé told me.

Two white guys. They are neighbors.

One has legal trouble. The other is a lawyer.

It's a nice Saturday afternoon. The one that's in legal
trouble sees the lawyer outside watering his plants. They
chat for a little while. Neighbor shit. He got a little advice.

The next day that troubled neighbor received an invoice
for $175.00. Even.
Consultation fee.

True story. Do you understand what just happened? Ok so you understand how white people work. What's it worth to you?

Are you great at giving advice? If yes, why are you giving it away for free? White people are so good at selling shit they started a whole new job called *"Life Coach"!*

A Life Coach is a person who you go to for great advice. When I first heard that shit I was like-*"That's Me!"* I'm a Life Coach by nature so I can just start calling myself that and charging right? Wrong! White people made it up and made a killing doing it. So much so, that, now you have to *GET CERTIFIED* to do it. So wait! Ya'll really just told me I gotta come to ya'll school or take ya'll program just to **GIVE GOOD ADVICE**? Hilarious! That's white people for you honey. That's why I love to learn from them. I take all their shit and use it to my advantage. When you know better, you do better.

My point is, everything you possess is of value to someone, somewhere. Let me break this down further.

If you want to sell your hair you could get it made into a wig for cancer patients (no matter the grade, as long as it's healthy). I've always wanted to donate my hair to an organization like "Locks of Love". If you're from India, you could put it on welts and sell it for hundreds of dollars in the black community.

If you can sing well, not only could you put out platinum selling albums, but you could also win on a smaller scale like background vocals, an event singer or lounge singer.

If you can cook, please call me because I'll buy a plate, if it's good.

Is your house clean? Would you like to clean other people's houses? You could sell that service.

Can you sew? Have you ever thought of being a seamstress? You could repair and tailor. Or you could have your own line of custom event pieces.

I'm just going to keep it real. I've seen people sell pictures of their feet. A lot of these dudes with all these mixtapes could just sell the songs to bigger artists and make way more than what they're making now.

There's a market for everything. Trust me.

Who's Worthy?

This was my problem for far too long. I was always feeling like I was asking for too much or shooting too high. Never. No such thing. You have to believe in yourself and your product just that much that you'll charge what you think you're worth.

In the 1990's Jimmy Iovine, co-founder of Interscope Records, offered Master P $1 million. That was in the 90's! Right now today they're selling their souls for far less. He turned down the money and went the independent route. He counted on himself and his team. All he had was the buzz he started with just $10,000. Today, with no recently charting music, movies, or clothing in the past 10 years he's still worth almost $400 million. Half of you millennials probably have no idea of who he is except that Kodak Black mentioned him and they had a little disagreement. I mentioned him in a previous chapter now I want you to look him up. It'll make more sense when you educate yourself on the topic. That's your homework.

Remember I told ya'll I worked for the #1 Urban Radio station in the country? I interned there for 6 months. They hired me the day before I graduated from college. I was so ecstatic like- *"Yes! I just got my 1st job as a college grad and it's at the radio station! I'm rich!"* Chile, I was making an embarrassing $8/hr. Even with the 14-16 hours I worked on the regular I could barely afford to even get my ass out of bed for work. Silly me, when I was offered the job, not once did I think to ask how much I was getting paid or the job expectations. I was expecting to get my first check and it be about $2500! Laughing my ass off! I got that check like- *THIS AIN'T ENOUGH.* And they were like- **MAKE IT ENOUGH!** Hilarious!

I loved it the first year and a half. I was just happy to be there and they capitalized off that. Several things were coming into play here. I had a criminal record so I was grateful to just get the damn job. So I felt I owed them something. My program director knew that because I'd confided in him when he hired me because I knew I couldn't pass a background check. I feel he preyed on that. Another thing at play here was always constantly being told "you have to work hard for anything you want in this life" and at the radio station they believed, "you have to pay your dues".

Shit maybe I could pay my dues if ya'll paid me more. That's how I saw it. I had to stop allowing people to tell me that "things take time". That's a way for them to string you along in most cases. And I had to stop letting people tell me— you have to work hard and sometimes take less. That's not true! That's never been true! Well, let me rephrase...Sometimes you have to give a little to get a little. Then sometimes you have to give a lot to get a lot. But then some people give a little to get a lot. Some are so talented they don't even have to give anything and they get it all. No matter which one you are, you didn't take a loss. But BLACK PEOPLE teach their children that sometimes you gotta give a lot and only get a little. That, my friends, is called taking a loss. Don't find yourself always on the losing end. Pay attention.

But I believed in my dreams that much that I would take that kind of pay cut when I had just left a job at the hospital making $16/hr. I quit to finish school so I could potentially make more! *Ironic.* But I figured it was "part-time" (which turned into LIFETIME) so I could just work two jobs and still have access to this opportunity to follow my dreams. Be careful. People and jobs prey on that.

So here I was on the night show with the best radio personality ever, Greg Street, and they started moving me around. When I say I board-op'd/produced on every show on that station and on the "talk" station. You would think they would have offered your girl a dollar or something. They offered me zip zero- stingy with deniro. I didn't know how to ask either. Such a shame. But wait—there's more.

A new lady came in, she was from New York. She was bold and feisty and she was beautiful. I hated that she was coming to our station because I'd seen our PD do nothing but recruit powerful women from different stations around the country and try to berate and disparage them. But I just wanted to be on her show because a producer position with a salary was open. I manifested it. I worked on her show for 8 months as "Acting Producer". They didn't give me the position. They brought in her old producer from New York. He had 20 years experience and they had a vibe. I was crushed. I was 23 years old and fighting for a dream and I was just over it. I was so hurt and so miserable. She was apologetic and said she didn't know. But my PD had no remorse. It's business. But for me it was personal.

They'd taken me off my show with Street where I felt comfortable and had moved me all around the station. Then I worked the PRODUCER POSITION (same low pay) on the midday show a whole 8 months! 8 months! 8 months! Then they hired someone else for the job. **THEN ASKED ME TO TRAIN HIM.**

Yep. I trained him, but not to the best of my ability. In fact I may have left out a few key strokes that I'd learned over time. Shit he had more experience than I did. I figured he'd be okay.

He didn't last a month.

Guess who they called.

Now let me point this out. The wonderful Kendra G. was a colleague of mine at the time. You might know her from the "Chicago Morning Takeover" on 107.5 or "Good Day Chicago". She knew of the problems I was having and she offered me kind words and some knowledge.

She told me to read *"The Game of Life and How to Play It"* by   Florence Scovel Shinn and *"How to Win Friends and Influence People"* by Dale Carnegie. I only read one… and I still didn't listen.

Laughing my ass off! I'm sorry Kendra! But thank you honey!

The PD called me into his office and offered me the position I'd been waiting so long for. And I turned it down. That's right. Then the host asked me and I said I couldn't.

My heart and mind was out of it. Once they played me and did all that, I went back to the night show and I refused to leave for anything. So when they asked me back I said I had a day job that paid more. Now had I listened to the advice in those books I would have taken it and used it to my advantage like white people do.

But instead I acted like a ~~nigga~~ and let my feelings get in the way. Do I regret it? Not at all. I looked in the PD's eyes and smirked at the fact that I was no longer going to be played and there was nothing he could do about it. Why did I do that? Because I took it personally. It wasn't. Everyone loved me, but I was new to the business and they wanted more experience. They were thinking short term. And that's just what they got. Needless to say, the middays didn't do well and the host was let go.

Had I been her producer I would have been canned as well. So I made the right decision, some would say, 'cause I still had my job, but had I been her producer on radio I might have been able to leave with her and become a producer on one of her HGTV shows. Who knows?

I won't know because not only did I not know my worth (because I should have asked for more money to even be "acting producer"), but I also let my feelings get the best of me when I finally got what I wanted. There's also the part where I was only looking at possibilities from a limited point of view. That's why this book is important. You didn't pick up this book by chance. Your time is upon you.

When you go into any situation where you're selling something, first do your market research. You sell hair? What's the going rate for a bundle of hair? I bet everyone that sells weed knows how much it's going for in their area and other states. You should know the same about your product, even if *YOU ARE THE PRODUCT*. If you're applying for a job you need to know upfront which position you want and how much people in that position make. Consider your years of experience and additional skills. Consider your schooling. Go in there prepared. Know what you're willing and unwilling to take. Get your number in mind. Get a counter offer in mind. And if you can't get exactly what you asked for, be prepared to walk away or be prepared to prove yourself. The choice is yours.

That's the crazy part to me. I finally looked up the standard radio producer's annual salary and it was less than $60,000 in Atlanta and less than $40,000 in most other places. But the morning show producer at the time was only making $30,000 so I was really ready to go then cause I didn't even know what I was shooting for there. They were robbing her blind. I know that because the white man they brought from New York hit them for $60,000.

Turns out, it was just a stepping stone. Like Egypt Sherrod told me in those months I worked on her show, *"You know what Nonie. Maybe radio isn't it. Maybe you're just here to meet the person that's going to take you to the next place on your journey to where you need to be!"*

She was right. I was letting the drama of radio side track me from the ultimate goal. But GOD was on my side. One night my colleague (at the time) and author, Shanae Hall asked me to help her with a meet and greet. Tyrese was doing a book signing with the radio station and we had to finalize the plans. We met up on the set of *Fast and Furious 7*. The next day I had a job in film. I quit the radio station before long. It was barely 3 years and I started my new life, making 3 times as much. I haven't looked back since. That's another book.

But on your journey I want you to carry something with you, **YOU ARE WORTHY**! And in the words of Young Dolph, *"Get paid young nigga, GET PAID!"* Know your worth. I'm preparing to sit down for a major deal in a few weeks. Just know- *I'M COMING FOR IT ALL!*

And if you're still lost in this sub chapter maybe this will help. You just read all that I went through at that radio station and when I was in a car accident and finally came back to work, they wouldn't work with me on my doctor's appointments. I would come in with appointment letters because I was still bleeding from the trauma of the accident, I had a flashing light going off in my right eye from the concussion, and I had go to the chiropractor cause I had surgery on my leg. It was always, "We'll see."

After all that I'd done at that job and all the complimentary hours I'd worked, that's how they did me. After I'd gone up for several different higher positions and was sabotaged, I couldn't catch a break. Then when I quit and went on to do production on movies someone blocked me from the station's social media. I guess they got tired of watching me win! Haha!

It's important you grasp this because young people are constantly taken advantage of in the workplace, especially young black people. You deserve what you want. If the job is offering $9/hr and you want $12/hr you better stake your claim and bring a body of proof as to why you feel you deserve it. It's time to get our piece of the pie. If I were a white person I would own that radio station cause I would have sued the socks off their asses. But I didn't know. No one around me knew. But now I do so I'm telling you. Do your homework.

You have to worry about your bottom line because at the end of the day it's about the bottom line and that's the bottom line.

Paper Trail

"One thing about white people, they fight you with that black and white baby- *ink and paper."*

That's what everyone was telling me when I was preparing to take my former business partner to court. So this is a story about how you need to always make sure your paperwork is right.

In the summer of 2017, I took $50,000 out of my personal account and started ***Singleton Express Transpo,***

LLC. with my brother. I was super excited! I'd always wanted to start a family business and my brother had a viable skill so why not? We did a family deal.

No paperwork.

I put up the money so it was my company, but I would be his 50/50 partner or exit the company as an owner and just buy a truck to run under the company— *after the return on my investment.* I did all the paperwork and paid for everything. I bought a truck and put my brother in a life changing position. For two months I was on the West Coast waking up at 5am to get a head start on business in the Central and Eastern time zones.

I was dispatching loads, doing invoices for factoring, keeping up with taxes and compliance. My brother was driving. The "brand new" truck had to be put in the shop twice and I paid for it. In just under 3 months my brother decided he was going to keep my truck because I wouldn't give him an extra $1500 for spending money on his honeymoon after he'd just spent $10,000 of company money on his wedding, honeymoon and other frivolous shit. How much did I make in all this time and spending? $1600!

True shit! I got the paper trail to prove it!

When we got into a text argument he said, *"I built this company!"* I so desperately wanted to understand what he thought was built for him to even say that. It had barely been 3 months! Laughing my ass off! Then he said he was keeping the truck because it was in his name. Now here is what I want ya'll to pay attention to.

When we got the truck I didn't think we were getting it for another few weeks so I was in the car smoking weed while my brother was in the building letting them know we weren't getting the truck so cancel the process. I thought we'd agreed to go to the Midwest because Texas didn't have much within our budget. I got out the car because it was taking a while. When I walked in, his name was on the paperwork for the truck. The audacity! Like the money for the truck isn't coming by way of a check with my signature on it. I made them change it to the company name. I'm the company according to the paperwork honey. I had to explain that to my brother. I told him on several occasions before we even got that far into the dysfunction- **let's sit down with a lawyer**. He refused, but I didn't. I got some legal advice and had to go my separate ways. We had no paperwork between us. We barely had a verbal contract, shit. All we came up with was that no one would get paid for the first month. At the end of that month we would add up the money and half would stay in the account and the other half we would split. Seemed simple enough. But see the way my brother's spending habits are set up— he wanted more than his fair share.

He felt that as long has he was driving, there was money. True, but he forgot about the bills associated with running the company and he most certainly forgot about the bill the company owed to me- *50 RACKS!* So I had to tell him one too many times, I've never lived check to check and I'm not going to run this company like that! He was going behind my back and transferring money, going to ATM's and shit, wiring money, and just flat out misusing unauthorized business funds.

I'll never forget the time we were waiting for our money to clear to the account. It was supposed to clear that night at 9pm. Don't you know at 7pm he went to a spot and with $100 left on our bank card, he spent $70 on CRAWFISH! Yooooo! I can't make this up! I understand he thought he'd have more money by the end of the night, but then it didn't come and he was pissed because he barely had enough gas to drop off a load. And if you're not running- you're not making money. It came by the next afternoon, but you missed maybe another $1200. So do you see how that thinking can be detrimental? Anything could happen!

That's why I told you the names of the those two books Kendra G. told me about. Had my brother read them, maybe he wouldn't have put a multi-million dollar idea turned corporation in jeopardy. He was moving off emotion. And it was directed towards me because he refused to see what he was doing. But because I read those books (hint, hint) I also see how I was wrong in this situation. It's a problem I've always had, even in 4th grade when I was selling lollipops. I asked my homegirl to help me. She did. She brought the money back. I gave her half. My grandmother explained to me why I was wrong. She was the one that bought the box of lollipops! If anything I should have given her half. Of the $8 I made in that one run I owed my grandma at least $4 so she could make her money back for what she spent for the box and profit $2. Then I should have made $3 and gave my homegirl $1. So I'm not an idiot. I've been knowing how to handle business for a long time- *AND YET AGAIN I LET EMOTIONS GET IN THE WAY OF BUSINESS.*

Yea he's my brother and I wanted him to be an owner, but I had to protect my investment. Yes, he's the one picking up and dropping the loads. But I did all the paperwork: for the business, the truck, the bank account, the insurance, the compliance, the factoring, the brokering and dispatching the loads. And even if I didn't do any of that- **I PUT THE MONEY UP! I BOUGHT THE TRUCK!** But for some reason he felt he built this barely 3 month old company that I'd been working on for the last 6 months just to get it up and running. That's because he doesn't understand business. **And that's because we're family.**

He made a comment about how I would be finding loads and would be able to go back to sleep while he was on the road. Ok. And that's the life I can afford. Think about it. At least I got up earlier than you and found your loads and checked in with you and submitted the paperwork for the companies to get paid. Cause I've worked a lot of places and the owner of the company didn't do any of that. I didn't even know who they were. What I mean by that is- Nigga if I'm my own boss and you're your own boss why the hell you watching what I'm doing, but can't do your part right? I'm getting us twice the market value for the load and you can't get it there on time, but you're mad cause I can go back to sleep? 'Cause that's how niggas think! Don't be like niggas! Play your role.

When he was driving for the white man he had no complaints. He was on the road for 2 weeks straight with only a weekend separating him from another two weeks on the road. He was making 32 cents per mile. But when he was working for me I treated him better than I treated myself. I was negotiating loads for $3.50 per mile, he didn't want to go cross country so I just ran him in Houston and the surrounding areas- AND HE HAD WEEKENDS OFF! It's like, what more do you want? You had it made in the shade.

And of course I'm simplifying things. I left out the part where he blew my UPS contract BY OVERSLEEPING. I left out a lot that happened, but I have a paper trail of about 90 things he did that were fireable offenses (half of them are times he stole money).

Somewhere in the middle of all of that I told him I had 'til the top of the year to see some type of turn around or I would be pulling my investment and thereby, dissolving the company. Everything went to shit in November, barely 3 months in to operations and making almost $40,000. But that was just God's way of protecting me. See had it been even a year in and this happened, it would have been a harder fall. I think it's safe to assume he would have still been fucking up and it would have been harder to walk away 'cause he would try to stick me for my paper. So I'm grateful.

I never tried to act like I was the boss. I always tried to make him feel equal meanwhile in this fool's head he deserved more than me. Baby, a driver comes a dime a dozen. A young black woman with the tenacity, ambition, know how, and gumption to make some shit like this happen— is RARE! But that's how the game goes. And that's my brother.

But even with all he stole from me, I still came out on top 'cause I got the business out of it. He went to jail briefly and it was the talk of the town and of the family. Of course I was painted as "the bad guy"! But no one knows the whole story because I've refused to even speak on it. Why? Most of the people talking about my business couldn't even understand it if I spoke in business terms. I'm a humble soul, but the things taking place in my life are above a lot of your pay grades. So why even engage in some gossip to defend myself with a bunch of bitches who barely have an 8th grade education? I'm more concerned with keeping my business going. Seriously, once the police recovered my truck you wouldn't believe the condition. The side door was dented. All four of the truck's batteries were missing. All my brand new tires and rims were missing. All the radio and air conditioning wiring was pulled out. Somebody was hard up. So now you can add *vandalism* to *embezzlement*.

But God is always good to me. The same company I intended to use to repair it, towed it from Houston to New Orleans. They fixed a few small items- AND BOUGHT THE TRUCK! I was praising God because I thought I had a very long road ahead with it.

To this day, I don't know what happened. But I'm not fixated on that. I had to do the only thing I know how to do — **KEEP MOVING FORWARD**. I bounced back and business is booming! My motor carrier company just partnered with a brokerage so it's safe to say things are going well. Owner Operators get at me. Let's just say he's been compensated for his knowledge. Plus I get $30,000 back from the secured loan I took out once I'm done paying it off. So I only paid $20,000 in the end. I paid more for college so I should have done this a long time ago. I think I still owe the school a couple hundred dollars for them to even send the piece of paper. *Rolls eyes*

Paper. Paper trail. Paper work. Make sure you have that.

So if you've been paying attention to the lessons so far you can spot all the problems and you know we as black people do this shit more often than not.

We just witnessed everything taught in chapters 1, 2, and 5! And just like I said- *we always do it the wrong way*! So now you believe me.

But of course I was depicted as the bad guy and word on the street is I do bad business deals. Shiiiiddd… I feel I offered the deal of a lifetime. He renigged. I didn't bother to tell anyone the whole story. Why, when I can put it in the book and make them buy the book to get the tea? See! Just utilizing some of the things I learned from white folks. Hahaha!

Luxury Tax

When I think back on the times me and my brother had, "building" this business "together", I'm happy! For a while I'd been wanting to just do something. I had the money. I just didn't know what to do. I wanted an investment property. I let people around me scare me about being a home owner with tenants aka landlord. I wanted to start an online boutique with my sisters and a natural cosmetics line with my homegirl. I wanted to start a food truck with my girl Brandie. I moved to California and started making hats and shirts with some friends, they were unprofessional so I parted ways. I told you 'bout me selling lollipops in 4th grade and I sold po'boy lunches with a snack and drink in 10th grade. I've always been this person! *I'm not a businessman, I'm a business, man*.

I always knew who I was, but I didn't have any real experience as a business owner under my belt. Singleton Express did that for me! I saw the rise and the fall. It took away that fear of investing in myself and taking a chance on me. This was the first time— *I BET ON ME AND I WON!* That has given me new found confidence. Now I've been making small investments into other up and coming companies. It's been amazing! I've grown in a way that I understand who I am and the power I possess. It's only right that I tax for access to it.

My sister Meekie said to me one day, *"You've always done everything you said you would. There hasn't been one time you haven't accomplished what you set out to do."* She explained how rare it is. But until this very moment I didn't equate rare to valuable.

I literally came up with a business idea. I didn't know anything about it. I found someone who did and I put my money up to open the multi-million dollar company. That company has consistently made money. By anyone's standards— **I'M A SUCCESS!** Some would call me a Republican. You'll catch it in the morning! Haha!

I've given you countless examples of situations I've been in and come out on top of. I can talk to you about it all day for free, but I'm not showing you how to do it for free. But as you learned at the top of this chapter, I can charge you just to talk to you about it. You bought the book didn't you? That's how valuable I am.

That's how valuable you are as well. The other side has already figured it out and they are capitalizing off us everyday. We don't need a seat at the table. We need our own table.

When you recognize your power and figure out what you sell, let me tell you how easy it will be to make money. We like to club on the weekend. Why? It's a chance to get out the house. We can hear music and dance. We can have a few drinks and mingle. You could do that shit at your house, but it's the experience. Who's providing the experience? The owner of the building hired a DJ, a promoter, and some people to serve you. You don't even notice they charged you money to park, money to get in, then charged you for drinks. Some of you were charged for separate seating because you think you're a Very Important Person and in that section, the club charged you $200 or more for a bottle of liquor that's only $30-$40 in the store. They charged you for their ability to make that experience happen for you. Then they taxed you because they can.

That's how most businesses and business people think.

People don't pay you for what you know. They pay you for what you do with what you know. You are valuable. Your knowledge and know-how is valuable and your time is valuable.

That's how the rich think. Remember Mariah Carey sued her ex-boyfriend for $5 million as an "inconvenience fee" for wasting her time? Need I say more?

Conspectus

So many people miss out on an opportunity because there's not a check involved. Sometimes a relationship is better than money. But now it's time to only seek out opportunities where you can benefit in some way. Figure out all the ways you can benefit with or without money involved. Think about the many ways it could still turn into exactly what you want or need. After all of that if it still doesn't seem worth it- *IT AIN'T WORTH IT!*

I can say that because now I look back and realize all the ways I still had a chance of getting where I wanted to go no matter which road I took. I now realize my limited thoughts contributed to what was already trying to hold me back in the real world.

For example, the radio station didn't pay much but that's because they felt we could figure out ways to make our own money off their name and not just with payola either. That was only one part. You could build your own buzz off their name and start doing parties. I could have created my own site and been like Karen Civil. I'm only telling you that because sometimes we want cake, but when God hands us flour, eggs, and milk we get mad. I didn't understand that then. I just wanted a decent wage for my consistent work. But that's not really how *this* game is played. So I had to switch up my thinking. It took me a while to catch on, but once I got it, I ran with it. I didn't blame them, I leveled up.

Someone could take the hand you were dealt and win with it.

Sometimes we are the problem and what you don't know can hurt you.

I had to learn *"the game of life and how to play it"*.
Hint. Hint.

Read that book.

Chapter 9: Build A Community

"It takes a village…" ~ *African Proverb*

In "Black neighborhoods", when we start to see buildings change and white people start walking around, we know one thing- *GENTRIFICATION IS UPON US!* **Gentrification.** The process of renovating and improving a house or district so that it conforms to *"middle-class taste"*. Middle class taste, huh? They build Trader Joe's, Jamba Juice, LA Fitness and Starbucks- *White people's taste.*

So if we can identify that, it must mean "White neighborhoods" have a distinctive look. Ok. Well, do our neighborhoods have a distinctive look? Of course they do. Most of them look like *"The Projects"* or close. Dead grass or no grass. Buildings that could fail code inspection, homes that haven't had any upkeep in years, trash everywhere and crimes happening that we claim "we ain't seen" is what one would imagine. A breeding ground for more crime and confusion is what it leads to. It's all connected.

If we don't create an environment that is conducive for productivity, achieving success will always be like winning the lottery for black people— *1 in a million chance*.

It starts at home. In-house. In the community.

We don't take care of our community because we all are trying so hard to get out of there. That's working against us and we don't even know it.

One thing White people will do is step up in the community- and not against one another. They work together.

Quick story.

My sister would always get these tickets in the mail. Stop light tickets. In other words, she runs red lights. I'm not over exaggerating when I say she had a table full of notices. One day I called her like, "What's going on with you? These tickets are piling up!" Her response was, "I'm not paying that. It's illegal and they can't enforce it."

So I hit her with the, "Okay girl. You've been living around those white folks out there in Jefferson Parish far too long. When your license gets suspended you'll see you can't bend the rules." Her response changed my whole perspective, "We don't have red light tickets in Jefferson Parish— the white folks voted against it."

Think about that! We're all in Orleans Parish being harassed and robbed of our coins, the poor getting poorer. But just a few minutes away in Metairie them white folks said they ain't paying that shit and they stuck together and the city took most of the cameras down. The ones that are up don't work or just serve as street surveillance.
Wow!

Now don't you all go ripping up your tickets at once. She still had to pay an $1800 fee to get a boot off her car one night leaving work. Hahaha! Orleans Parish was hunting her down. I wouldn't want you to go to jail or anything. Especially because that's the leading cause of the break down of our communities.

Modern Day Slavery

What if I told you slavery never ended? What if I told you they just repackaged it and re-distributed it? What if I told you, that's part of the reason Black communities fail today?

Now what if I told you Black people make up 13% of the U.S. population, but account for 34% of all jail inmates and 37% of all prison inmates? These are not trick questions. These are all factual statistics that you can google. In 2014, there were 2.2 million inmates in prison.

How many were black? 814,000! These are just the statistics for men. Let's talk about women. In 2011 there were 1.6 million women in prison- 23% were black. That's 368,000! Come on now! No, we're not the highest percentage as the media would have you believe. But- that's still 1.2 million Black women and men in prison in 2014. I didn't give you jail statistics nor did I give statistics of our youth that are in and out of jail.[19]

And for what?

Well, for business purposes. If you're a McDonald's employee or your little league team just bought new uniforms or you just bought a new car and need a license plate, nine times out of ten- a person in jail made it for you. No need to pay little Chinese kids $2 a month to work in a sweatshop making Jordans when they can ship the factory to one of the many prisons here and get it done for FREE!

Trust me it's not free. Someone's paying for it. Let me tell you how we're all being played. Most prisons today are PRIVATE! What that means is- you and I could open a prison if we chose to. It's government funded. They pay, on average, around $65,000 per year per inmate. With the rate that black people are in and out of prison and catching life sentences- *IT'S BIG BUSINESS TO OWN A PRISON!* So much so, that prisons have actually threatened to sue their states if they don't help keep the prisons filled. This is a fact that can be googled. Please look it up.

Think about it. If the government has $65,000 to pay *Privately Owned Prisons* to house, feed and provide medical care to inmates, they could make college free. Healthcare for "free" citizens could be free. But it's not. Why not? Because if you have to struggle for basic necessities and you already live in poverty- that's the recipe for a life of crime- AND *CRIME PAYS, just not for you unfortunately*.

I know what you're thinking, "Omg! I'm outraged! How can they do this?" Well, do you remember the 13th amendment? The one that freed the slaves? Ratified on December 6, 1965, the amendment states, "Neither slavery nor involuntary servitude, except as a punishment for crime whereof the party shall have been duly convicted, shall exist within the United States, or any place subject to their jurisdiction.

No slavery shall exist, EXCEPT AS A PUNISHMENT FOR CRIME! So in other words, they just found another way of enslaving you, and improved on the tactics they use to bait you in!

But it gets worse. So you get out of jail, now it's hard for you to get a job. So now what? You're back to thinking of ways to *"hit a lick"* and that my friend is going to land you back in jail. But there's more to it. You're teaching your kids that going back and forth to jail is "normal" and that getting a decent job so that you can afford the lifestyle you want— is hard or impossible!

It's sad. My father had been in the Louisiana State Penitentiary, Angola, for almost 30 years. On my last visit I almost broke down. I saw a group of kids all dressed up. They were just outside talking and laughing. They had artwork and gifts their dads made. The women had similar arts and craft gifts. In that moment, I realized "prison life" was normal for these people as it had been for me all these years. Some women even met their partners while on prison visits to see relatives. It's a culture.

When my brother was 16 he "took a charge" for his friend's dad- A GROWN ASS MAN! He bonded out, but that charge stuck with him. When he was 18 years old he wanted to go to a tech college for auto body repair. He needed *Financial Aid*, but the FAFSA wouldn't go through because he had a criminal record- *DRUG CHARGES SPECIFICALLY.* So that led to him not being able to go to school. So he stayed in the streets. He eventually caught another drug charge that sent him to jail for 5 years! He got out in 2 years. Life went on. He continued down this road until he was facing 10 years. Does this all sound familiar to you? I'm sure you all know SEVERAL people that this applies to, many who didn't even attempt to go to school. But do you remember when I told you my father has been a slave for almost 30 years? Maybe my brother simply wants to follow in his footsteps.

It's a trap, I promise. They set you up and then take away all your rights and earning potential (unless you open your own business). The craziest part is then- YOU'RE LOCKED IN HERE! Not only are you imprisoned, but when you get out- you can't even get a passport to travel and see the world without stipulations.

Don't be so alarmed honey. Slavery is nothing new. Look up police badges and slave patrol badges. The exact same!

Prison is the plantation. They use Slave Patrol to capture you and lock you away to work for free and they get paid top dollar on all of it. That's why the police don't care if they kill you in cold blood. It's because you're a threat to them alive and free, but you're worth BILLIONS to them incarcerated or dead.

Raising The Kids

Let me just piggy back off the last sub chapter. Staying out of jail is crucial, especially when you think about how we've glamorized it to the point that it is heavily ingrained and deeply rooted within our culture. We have normalized it. The kids want STREET CRED! They want to earn their STRIPES!

It's like a *"Rite To Passage"* for young black men. You're not a man until you have passed through the prison system. This is an unspoken standard in a lot of black communities that we have to destroy!

One of my best friends has an older brother who's always been in and out of jail. During the last trial he was sentenced to 10 years. Her mama threw him a "Going Away Party"! Are you serious? I didn't get a party when I went to college or finished college. I didn't get a party when I moved to California because I had a job offer that would land me at Warner Brothers Studios. Barely got a, "Good job!" "I'm proud of you!" No one made it a point to come visit me or send me money when times got hard, yet WE DO THIS FOR INMATES EVERYDAY! So why wouldn't our kids want to be inmates?

Inmates get 3 meals a day, free room and board, they get books and they can go to school to get a GED. Some have received college degrees in jail. You can go in and make friends and even join a gang if that's your thing. There's a basketball court and gym. It's LIT! That's how we sell our kids on going to jail when we don't give them the tools to succeed. Going to jail is easy.

But what kinds of crimes are these kids committing to end up in jail? The top crimes of juvenile delinquents are: THEFT, ASSAULT, DRUG ABUSE, and DISORDERLY CONDUCT. So what I take from that is we don't provide, so our children start stealing. Or we give what we can, but we're not teaching them to be grateful for what they have so they always want what they see on TV and when we can't meet it— they steal.

The fact that they are out here assaulting people shows we don't teach them how to handle their issues with communication. We are just perpetuating violence when we get physical with them instead of simply explaining things.

Drug Abuse. You know it's such a shame for people to go to jail for abusing drugs. It's truly a disease that stems from emotional and mental issues that we can't handle and haven't been taught positive ways to cope with. That's an unfortunate plight to pass down to your kids. All of this is a combination of disorderly conduct. It starts with us, the ELDERS!

If we don't correct it who will? No one! Here's a quick story to show you the importance of having positive representation and how important it is for those of us who make it to come back and clean up things.

When I was in 10th grade I attended McDonough 35 High School in New Orleans, Louisiana! Threeeeeeeee Fiiiiiiiiiive! See! I still have to do the call when I mention it. Unfortunately, it's not the Charter School it once was. But when I was there it was all about *Black Excellence*. I was a part of this program called *"Peace By Peace"*! We were a group of students who would come together to plan out and implement tactics for curbing the violence in the schools, hoping it would stop further violence than what already existed in the community.

I had so many folders at my house, piles and piles of paperwork for me to read. The packets were from the research done by the state. I was horrified! The stories of crime and passion had me crying! You gotta think about it. I was always hearing the horror stories of crime, but I didn't know first hand what was going on because I had not experienced it directly. But there was a clear consensus across the board.

Whenever the question of, *"What can be done?"* came up **they all agreed**:

"Don't do anything. Let them keep killing each other and soon enough they will eliminate the problem for us [themselves]."

I was sick to my stomach. I cried a lot and I told my stepmom what was said and she explained to me, *"You can't save them all and you can only do your part. If you feel you can help— do that. Don't worry about who doesn't believe these kids can make a change."*

That was in 2005. Ten years later in 2015 I launched my non-profit mentoring program, *"DREAM LIFE ACADEMY"*! Why? Because I made it out. I made the plan, I implemented it and IT WORKED! So now I'm going to do the same with children across the country and eventually *ACROSS THE WORLD*.

With my program we teach the youth about valuing themselves, healthy self-esteem, hygiene, preparing small meals, etc. But the part I love the most is that we *TRAVEL* with them. I plan to take them *ABROAD* real soon. I realize that our children need a change of scenery to open their minds.

The program is for at-risk youth, ages 9 to 18. We will teach them more along the way. By the time they are seniors in high school they will have all the necessary tools to succeed. They will know what direction they want to go, be it college, trade school, or workforce. They will have been to at least one other country and done a summer internship. That's how you build.

95

But as parents you can't forget to do your part like making sure they participate in extra curricular activities: band, sports, cheerleading, dance, art, choir, etc. This expands their minds, gives them purpose, teaches teamwork and social skills, and any of those skills could clearly open a door for them.

Group Economics

So let me be honest, I'm a group economics novice. I'm still new to this. I think I just found out, in 2012, the real meaning of group economics. Let me blow your mind too because it's never been broken down and our people perish because of lack of knowledge.

Do you remember when Martin Luther King, Jr. and his Civil Rights crew staged sit-ins and walked to work instead of riding the bus because they no longer wanted to be forced to sit in the back? It wasn't about Black people getting out there together and marching or chanting. That's just another way they showed their unity. It was really about hitting the businesses in the pockets!

Black people are and always have been major consumers, hell we low key still live off the barter system in the hood. But I talked about how much money we spend with "others" versus how much we make or put back into the neighborhood and it's crazy! It's been that way! In the 60's they would serve blacks but we had to eat out back. *Colored folk couldn't eat in the diner with the white folk.* Just like on the bus, we could ride the bus, but we had to sit in the back and leave the front for the whites. So what did we do? Well, shit, if I can't eat inside I'm not buying here! If I can't sit where I want I'm not riding with your transit system! The city and the businesses lost so much money! They made a financial decision to integrate! Remember that! The bottom line.

We, collectively, are a CASH COW! Marvel's Black Panther recently hit theaters. We all were so excited. So we were talking about going dressed up like AFRICAN KINGS AND QUEENS! Some people said they were going to dress up like Eddie Murphy's "Coming to America"!

I love that movie! I just read "Batman vs. Superman" was the franchise's top film, but Black Panther beat it in PRE-SALES which means the movie wasn't even out yet and was breaking records!

So all the Black people were eating it up. There was a rumored petition going around. The Black Community was "asking for" 25% of the proceeds to be allocated to programs in the black community. Tell me why some black people were saying, *"Damn we got a movie; when will we be happy?"* That's the old black way of thinking. **Inferiority complex.** We don't do that anymore. Not 'round these parts!

I'm like, let's be for real! You think Marvel really made Black Panther and dropped it during Black History Month for some type of *"Power To The People"* effect? No? That's what happened and we're happy! The company, however, did it that way for **THE MONEY**! It's genius! Yes, I know the back story of how this character came about so I know the cross reference, *BUT THE COMPANY DID IT FOR MONEY*! And asking for a percentage to go towards programs that benefit black people is not asking for too much! You know why? Because when WHITE PEOPLE have a hit movie they throw a dinner to celebrate! At that dinner the producers thank everyone! And sometimes they even DONATE MONEY TO A CAUSE, IN THE NAME OF THE PERSON(S) TO WHOM THEY CONTRIBUTE THEIR SUCCESS! It's us who constantly play it small. Companies make so much money off us not knowing our worth.

But you have just witnessed how GROUP ECONOMICS WORK!

Martin Luther King, Jr. made them feel the Civil Rights Movement in their pockets! We don't buy, they can't sell. Marvel made Black Panther for it's POCKETS! It was a great message nonetheless. Haha! Then when Black people realized how much money was being made off US SUPPORTING THE MOVIE— we decided they needed to dig in them pockets and put back into our communities!

But let me tell you a secret— *IT'S MUCH DEEPER!* I was reading this article on Blavity: *"How Black Millennials Can Practice Group Economics — Right Now"* by Raphael Wright. It changed my life. This article is already a year old so you know I feel so behind. But the way he breaks it down just opened my eyes to things I've seen work for White People. I'll give examples as I break it down Wright's article:

1.   Form a Money Kye pronounced "Keh"

"The term "keh" describes the Korean informal lending system where a community contributes a nominal sum of money into a pool that is loaned to a single person or family to help them get on their feet. Everyone who contributes in this system receives the pool at some point throughout the lending cycle and it never ends. This system allows a community to help their own on a regular basis. Today, people can form these types of money pools online with sites like eMoneyPool that will allow you to form a community fund for virtually anything."[20]

The Gist

In White America that's called A *MUTUAL FUND*.

A mutual fund is an *investment vehicle* made up of a pool of money collected from many investors for the purpose of *investing in securities* such as stocks, bonds, money market instruments and other assets.[21] So basically a group of 10 friends, family and/or colleagues put $10,000 together to make $100,000 to open a nail salon. You go further faster as a group.

2.   Invest in the Stock Market

"Black people have a minimal presence in the stock investing world because of the huge financial requirements to make a meaningful impact. But, what if communities pooled their funds together to invest as a group? This is very possible through investment groups or clubs. Investing

in stock is as simple as creating a brokerage through a discount broker like eTrade."[20]

The Gist

Three words. DOT COM BUBBLE! Google it! This has happened IN OUR LIFETIME MILLENNIALS! When we were kids, so many people got rich simply by investing money on a hunch that the internet would take off.

Let me tell you how ridiculous this shit is. My mama worked for Amazon in 2000. Their stock opened at $18 in 1997. Now it's $1696.35! She had the jump on it and didn't even know it. Imagine if, in 2000, she took half of her tax refund and bought shares in Amazon... That's going on around us everyday!

In 2001 my mom could have taken $1500 of her tax money and bought about 40 shares of Amazon's stock. If 2 more friends joined that would be $4500 and 120 shares. That would be $236,322. That would be $78,774 a piece and they did nothing, but let their money sit. Of course I'm over simplifying it, but it's also pretty simple.

3.   **Buy Real Estate**

"Nothing is more pivotal to group economic success than ownership of the land a community occupies. In America, African-Americans have one of the lowest percentages of land ownership. Again, working together and pooling our funds together, groups of black millennials can buy up many acres of land and do whatever they wish with it."[20]

The Gist

Gentrification. We see it all the time. We live in these neighborhoods, not owned by any of us, and White Folks just keep hiking up the rent to get you out and new money in. It's business. That's why all your favorite rappers are now talking about ***"Buy Back The Block"***.

But you have to buy the real estate and keep up with it. Quick story. I know someone who's mother left her and her sister a house. They didn't keep up with the taxes on it and an old white man went down to city hall and paid the (back) taxes, thereby owning the house. When he died his children wanted to settle all his debts. This was a house in **Historic Uptown New Orleans** off Baronne Street. It was worth $200,000 falling down. This white man got it for $300! His kids just wanted his money back, plus interest. It was all of $13,000 yet she nor her sister, who (by the way) got $150,000 from Road Home after Hurricane Katrina and never fixed the house up or paid the taxes, could come up with the money! THIS WAS A BLACK FAMILY with this kind of money and property being played with because we don't handle our business like we should. The good news is they made a GoFundMe and one of the cousins came forward to buy it! Thank God it could stay in their family. But look at that! We need to get our shit together and keep it together.

4.   Form Partnerships and Form Business Startups.

"Dame Dash said it best, "when you cop as a group, the bag is cheaper." By "copping," Dame is referring to a group of people forming a partnership to start businesses. The power of numbers are always visible in the entrepreneurial field. If we practiced this dynamic, there's nothing we can't accomplish in business."[20]

The Gist

White people will simply register a business. Once their kids turn 16 they start paying them through the business. By the time they are of age to leave the house they have a business that's been running for years that they've paid taxes on. They can get a line of credit for the business and that child is set! Meanwhile, the only people in the black community I've seen do this successfully are drug dealers. A few friends might peddle a little weed here and there and decide to put their money together to get a pound. Now they all are making more money and can buy more product so the business grows. Next thing you know everyone is rich! But the hairstylists can do it, the cooks can do it, the little boys that cut grass can do it, and the chicks that babysit can do it; join together and create a business. But of course you have to make sure your paperwork is right and duties are delegated and money is circulated.

5.   Consolidate Existing Businesses

"Another perspective of entrepreneurial partnerships is consolidation where two businesses merge to form an empire. The benefits are immense when experts can unite to build a larger company that will create more revenue opportunities."[20]

The Gist

You've seen this done so many times in White America. Mergers! All the old heads remember when AT&T bought BellSouth! Laughing my ass off! But you remember don't you? Okay then!

In 1999 with persistently low oil prices weighing on the industry, Exxon Corp [acquired] Mobil Corp in an $81 billion merger that created energy superpower **Exxon Mobil Corporation.**[22]

And there you have it! Wright helped me to understand it and now I've stated examples to help you understand it because we all should be doing it.

Conspectus

I've taught you how to build a community. I've given you examples. I've shown you the traps. I'm telling you what to do. I shared [that] I just learned some of this information. I want you to understand that it's not wrong to not know something, but it's wrong when you don't take advantage of the information that is available to you. You're walking around with a computer in your pocket. Do some research. It doesn't matter what the topic is. Research things that interest you and just keep reading no matter what topics come up.

But no matter what, keep digging into our history and keep learning the skills and gaining the tools necessary to take things to the next level.

Chapter 10: Be Fearless

"To get lost is to learn the way."
~ African Proverb

I love that proverb because it's so true. It represents how we can be so wrapped up in *"the problem"* that we can't see what it's teaching us. If you move to a new city you're bound to get lost. But every time you get lost, you learn which way to go. But as far as African Proverbs go they had a few that hit home for this chapter.

You always learn a lot more when you lose than when you win. ~ African proverb

You learn how to cut down trees by cutting them down. ~ Bateke Proverb

The wise create proverbs for fools to learn, not to repeat. ~ African Proverb

By the time the fool has learned the game, the players have dispersed. ~Ashanti Proverb

One who causes others misfortune also teaches them wisdom. ~ African Proverb

Instruction in youth is like engraving in stone. ~Moroccan Proverb

Ears that do not listen to advice, accompany the head when it is chopped off. ~African Proverb

Advice is a stranger; if he's welcome he stays for the night; if not, he leaves the same day. ~Malagasy Proverb

Traveling is learning. ~Kenyan Proverb[23]

I listed all of them so that you can see that BEING FEARLESS is less about fear and more about always being open to LEARN! Learning takes you places.

White people naturally appear fearless because they zip line and skydive. They swim with the sharks and travel to exotic countries alone. They go boating and surfing. I'm black. And the only thing I haven't done on that list is skydive. It's time to open our minds to all of the possibilities out there. There are people who grew up with a life you couldn't even imagine— good and bad. There are countries you've been told lies about that you just have to see! There are people waiting that you were meant to encounter on your journey in this life!

Quick story of how "FEARLESS" White People can be.

In Year 2000 (do ya'll still say that), I had a white homegirl I met through some church program that was helping black people get housing. You know white folks like to encounter struggling families in the hood. Ghetto Safaris! They learn a lot. Laughing my ass off. Her mom was friends with my mom.

Man, this girl wanted to spend the night at my house and I told her my siblings and I had to sing in the choir the next day at church. *A black church.* I was like, "You can come, but I don't want you to sit in the congregation alone." She was like, **"Oh no. That's ok. I'll come with you guys. I'll just sit with the choir."** "But you don't know the songs." **"Girl that doesn't matter. I'll just get up there and mouth the word *"Watermelon",* it goes with any song."** I did it a few times like- DAMN! SHE WAS RIGHT! Hilarious! I bet that little white girl got up to sing with the choir that Sunday at an all black church simply mouthing the word, *"watermelon"*!

Meanwhile, you're the next Whitney Houston or Beyonce, but you're scared to even tell people you can sing! What are you waiting for?

Even Indecision is a Decision

One of the main things that sets successful people apart from those who are not is— decision making! Your life is a sum of the decisions you've made up until this point. At any moment you can make a change. Successful people are quick to implement a new idea or strategy. You must act. Too many times we spend too much time on "trying" to figure out what to do instead of just doing it.

We all know the answers we seek.

Indecision is rooted in fear. You're afraid to make the wrong decision and THAT, my friend, is the worst decision you can make. I'm not saying you should act without thinking things through carefully or researching. I'm just saying your time of implementation from the initial idea to making it a reality should not take more than a few weeks to a few months. Why? Because you'll never know all you need to know until you **START**! At that point new ideas and questions will pop up that will help guide you, but if you're spending so much time "trying to figure it out" you're wasting valuable time and chances to win. You could have won by now!

My favorite story to tell about indecision happened in 2012. I'd been wanting to quit my job at the radio station and finally get into movies which was always the plan. I kept debating about it. Well, my friend DeQuan Jones came over and we were chatting at the pool. I said it again for the 1000th time- *"I'm thinking about quitting my job and going for my dream."*
My friend immediately busted my bubble, *"You still thinking about it? You were thinking about it last year at this same time! How long will you think about it?"*

So now I'm asking you. *"How long will you keep "thinking about it" or "trying to figure it out" before you move forward?"*

Someone is in need of what you're stalling on. Just like I stalled on putting this book out, but millions, if not billions, NEED THIS INFO!

Travel

If you don't take any other advice from this book, please take this sub chapter. It will change your life!

It doesn't matter what you read. It doesn't matter what information you think you know. It doesn't matter if you're the hottest in your city or state- **_YOU AIN'T SHIT IF YOU DON'T TRAVEL!_** Traveling opens your mind's eye to the world. Here in the United States of America we have been programmed to believe- _WE ARE THE WORLD_! I'm sorry to let you know- this country is small and insignificant compared to other people in the world. So let me break this down 'cause somebody about to get blessed.

I've always been a traveler. At first it was annoying because my mom was running from herself so she just kept picking up and moving us with no warning. Every few months we moved to a different city or state. We were lucky to complete a school year somewhere, but we knew we would never see those kids again. At first it hurt, then we got used to it. That's the sad part. But ultimately it opened my mind to the idea that I could continue to travel and go more places— BETTER PLACES!

The first thing I noticed when I started traveling was more people in this world look just like me than any other race. You read that right! Everywhere I've ever visited, especially the islands, was MAJORITY BLACK! But in America they would have you to believe the white man is the majority. He's actually the minority and dying out, but they know that already so google that fact later. That's another book.

I just got back from the Eastern and Southern Caribbean. It was eye opening and mind blowing. But something special happened. My fiancé and I started "sparking conversations". They told us how most of their countries gained independence as recent as 30-60 years ago. They got rid of the "colonizers" is what they said. But they gave us the formula. They said white folks move down to their islands and build vacation homes and rent them to tourists! You're probably like- "okay, but I ain't got no money for that"! Child please! They don't either. The conversion rate on the money in most of those places is anywhere from 2:1 to 5:1 to 7:1! What that means is, you can choose almost any one of those islands (independent) to move to and be 2 times as rich! If you have $5k now you have $10k. If you have $10K and you move to Trinidad, now you have $70k. So why not go build a home or business?

These are the secret tools that are being held on to. These are the tools that will set us free. We visited the Dutch Island of St. Maarten where a Black man put us up on game.

1.   He said he's Dutch. Yes he's a black man, but he said they don't really discuss race. That was unheard of because in our country EVERYTHING IS ABOUT RACE! *"In this country, American means White, everyone else has to hyphenate."* ~ *Tony Morrison*

2.   He makes $30K in Euros per month! That's over $40K USD! He said they have no poverty on their island and no government assistance. He feels it's directly connected.

3.   The schools there teach an international math and a MANDATORY 6 languages! Imagine going somewhere and seeing nothing, but black people who can, not only speak English, but can speak 5 other languages! EVERY ONE of them can!

4.   When I asked about his opinion of the U.S., he said the U.S. attempts to brainwash the people into "Patriotism" and never leaving, but on their island they want their people to be *CITIZENS OF THE WORLD*! They feel it's best to travel and see what's out there for you.

5.   Not only is he winning, he has 8 kids and the 4 oldest are business owners making over $20k in Euros a month. He put them on to what he does.

MAJOR KEY!

I felt like I had the **HOLY GRAIL** of all conversations! I want my kids to know 6 languages. I want them to grow up thinking "people are people" (even though I grew up thinking **Black People are Superior** and still do). I want them to be proud of their heritage. I want them in the company of individuals who's conversation is about international business and philosophy, not "a fight for civil rights or equal access to opportunities"! I owe that to them.

Business Model

The reason for the name of this subchapter comes from the idea that many of you will try your hand at entrepreneurship and it can be scary. Here's something I think I realized too late. To-Do lists, schedules, routines, and being organized ARE IMPORTANT. I didn't decide until I was 28 years old that I would start keeping a day planner. In my defense, I'm an artist. We go with the flow of life. Even when I worked in Corporate America I struggled with the time. I was always on time or early, but it was truly stressing me out. But it wasn't until I became an entrepreneur that I began to value a routine. And it's not what you think.

I used to wake up at 5:30am on the West Coast just to be up by 8:00am CST. By noon my time I would be done most days. That left me feeling like I'm not being productive for the rest of the day. So there I was, feeling like I'm not doing much because I don't "have a job"- *BUT I OWN THE COMPANY* and I'm getting it off the ground. But that's because of one important word- **"STRUCTURE"**! When you work for someone they've already done the leg work. They know what positions are needed and what position requires which skills, so when you go to work you have a clear cut day. You know what time to be there, what needs to be done before lunch, you take a lunch then you come back and do what you know needs to be done before the end of the day. You can create that in your own life and it doesn't have to be on the same time frame as a job would be— it just has to be organized!

You should run your life like a business. In order to do so you need a business plan. On that plan you will tell your mission statement and outline your goals. You will go further and break down those goals and give them a time frame. Then you will organize your days according to what needs to be done to further your progress. YES! You may do a lot of the same things each day. Don't look at it as mundane routine, look at it as a process. Everyday the builders show up to the same site until the house is built. You're not routinely doing something, you're BUILDING! All it takes is a little reprogramming!

You can apply business models to your love life and your finances. You should always have a goal in mind and you should only include people who fit the criteria of a good "business partner". It will save you a world of trouble. What successful relationship could you model yourself after, is there any information about how they make it work? Read it. Who's a person you would like to model your finances after? I know we all want to be rich, but if we're more specific it would sound like, "I want better credit. I want a higher salary. I want investments to make money for me while I sleep." All of those goals are attainable. Get to it.

Conspectus

Be fearless with your goals! People always ask, "What would you do for a living even if you weren't getting paid?" But they never tell you there are countless ways to make the most of that thing you love.

You don't have to be poor while following your dreams. Even if you want to be a school teacher you can live an extraordinary life. With just a high school diploma or a bachelor's degree in almost anything, you can teach English in a few different countries and live like royalty! You could teach English in Dubai! You co-create your life with God so use your imagination and DREAM BIG!

Look around you. It's not hard to live an ordinary life just routinely existing. It's not hard to live a life of struggling.. What's hard is being disciplined enough to work towards your goals everyday even when it doesn't look like anything is happening, even when there is no money coming in. In those time the fear is the greatest and we're tempted to retreat. Don't you dare turn back.

If you're going through hell, why would you stop? If God will bring you to it, she'll see you through it.

If you won't make a move because something bad might happen, nothing good will happen either.

Chapter 11: Rebuilding

"When a home is burnt down, the rebuilt home is more beautiful ." ~ Zulu Proverb

This chapter is all about rebuilding. If you mess up personal relationships there may be a chance of reconciliation. If you go off course in your finances there's a chance to rebuild as well. One of those is bankruptcy.

Bankruptcy is a legal status of a person or other entity that cannot repay debts to creditors. There are three main types of bankruptcy: Chapter 7, Chapter 11, and Chapter 13.

Chapter 7 provides for "liquidation" — the sale of a debtor's nonexempt property and the distribution of the proceeds to creditors. Chapter 11 provides for reorganization, usually involving a corporation or partnership. A chapter 11 debtor usually proposes a plan of reorganization to keep its business alive and pay creditors over time. Chapter 13 provides for adjustment of debts of an individual with regular income.[24] Chapter 13 allows a debtor to keep property and pay debts over time, usually three to five years.

Let's say you really messed up your finances and you don't know which option to pick, I'll break it down. Chapter 7 helps those that can just sell a few items and pay off the debt. Chapter 11 would be for those who need new management. If you're in financial trouble maybe that's not your strong suit and you need someone more skilled to help with something like that. Then Chapter 13 helps you keep all your stuff, but make a payment plan on the debt.

Many companies have done it and re-opened under another name. It's a common practice amongst business people, but the problem is the "working class" wants to spend like the 1 percent.

Now what I'm about to say goes back to "playing your role". Some of you have touched a little money and gotten "besides yourselves". Social media has gone to your heads and got y'all thinking you're living the lives of "the rich and famous"! You're not. Maybe the famous— but not the rich.

Remember what I told you. Black folks get money and buy houses, cars, and clothes. Shit they may even buy jewelry and hoes, but white people buy power! And who has the power in this country? They say, *"The People"*. But what they really mean is— *your vote*.

Voting Locally

I was 20 years old when I voted for President Barack Obama. That meant the world to me. It was about what it represented to the minds of millions of young Black kids. But now that Donald Trump is in office we're realizing now more than ever that "democracy" is far fetched, at least on a national level, but I'll go deeper into that statement later. Check this out, the city councilmen, mayors, district attorneys and judges, are all voted in by the people and are going to serve the interest of their political party. That's what Black people don't understand. All of us know someone doing hard time. We all know someone that's been harassed by the police. Shit until 2 weeks ago we were screaming #FreeMeek, but did you know the judge on his case can get voted out? Yes! You have to do your homework on the people running for local office. You can push and pull the strings to your liking because they need your vote, but they WILL SAY ANYTHING. Once they get in office you can HOLD THEM ACCOUNTABLE and/or force them out. We have rights!

I recently found out there are ALWAYS vacant seats in the city council and most of us qualify for the position. You could run as a State Representative to be in the House of

Representatives which is a part of congress. You could mess around and become a politician on some humbug shit. If you've ever voted before you've seen categories with just one name in the box. That person WINS AUTOMATICALLY (it seems). That could have been you or me. Black people need to understand that everyone in your community has to decide to be a leader. We're still waiting for A LOUD AND BOISTEROUS LEADER to be a martyr. That's dead! I be damned if I put my life on the line for us as a whole and be rolling over in my grave at Kanye West's recent statements. If I'm in the front, they know who to shoot. We all just need to do our parts on a local level and on the hush and watch how we come up.

But let's go DEEPER like I promised a few paragraphs back. Black people feel voting doesn't fix anything. We found out a long time ago with the *"Florida Ballots"* scandal of 2000 that this country will put in place who they want. But President Obama really made us believe in ***"The Power of The People"***. I miss him. Now we have Donald Trump in office and all the news outlets are just going crazy trying to figure out what the hell is going on and how to get him out of there before he burns this country to the ground with his racist antics. But it's funny because white folks are so pissed off that they're telling trade secrets. Ever heard of *Gerrymandering*?

Gerrymandering is a practice intended to establish a political advantage for a particular party or group by manipulating district boundaries. The resulting district is known as a gerrymander, however that word is also a verb for the process. The term *gerrymandering* has negative connotations. Two principal tactics are used in gerrymandering: "cracking" (i.e. diluting the voting power of the opposing party's supporters across many districts) and "packing" (concentrating the opposing party's voting power in one district to reduce their voting power in other districts).[25]

What do they mean by concentrating the opposing party's voting power in one district? Are you drawing lines around our communities and excluding us or are you somehow "herding" us into the areas of lower voting power?

113

In addition to its use in achieving desired electoral results for a particular party, gerrymandering may be used to help or hinder a particular demographic, such as a political, ethnic, racial, linguistic, religious, or class group, such as in U.S. federal voting district boundaries that produce a majority of constituents representative of African-American or other racial minorities, known as "majority-minority districts". Gerrymandering can also be used to protect whoever is currently in office.[25]

Yes. Re-read that. So basically you get the right to vote. Then go through Jim Crow with all these voting laws in place. Then they start slapping you with felonies to take your voting rights away. Please note that 2 Chainz heads a campaign called *"Respect My Vote"* that educates convicted felons on how "easy" it is to reinstate their voting rights. Currently, 39 out of 50 states offer it.[26] But just when you think you're in the clear, here they come with this gerrymandering bullshit.

That's what's crazy to me. They pull all these schemes to harass us and we still somehow get blamed for the division. But you all fall for it time and time again. I could not believe it when Keisha Lance Bottoms really had to do a run-off with that old white lady when she ran for mayor. I was sitting there like- *ARE THESE ~~NIGGAS~~ CRAZY*? It's been 60 YEARS of Black Mayors in Atlanta and just cause ~~niggas~~ got a lil money now they act like the forgot what's on the other side of that. How dare you?

So you're a Republican now? That's fine. I love Jay- Z and Nas' song *"Black Republican"* so I feel you. But let me break it down for those of you who don't really understand the difference.

When Democrats are in office, "they raise taxes on the rich" to have more money for "social programs" aka free shit like the career centers and Boys and Girls Clubs to help "the impoverished". Why? Well, because in this world, talent is distributed equally, but not opportunities. They feel we all deserve a chance.

When Republicans are in office, "they lower the taxes on the rich", it's by cutting social programs aka "free shit" to help the poor. Why? Because they operate on *"every man for himself"*. You could get it just like I got it, but you don't because you're lazy and make "poor" decisions. When taxes are lower, that opens the flood gates for them to buy up everything and get richer while raising prices on you—so you get poorer. BUT! When the flood gates are open that's also **PRIME** opportunity for you to come up as well. While Donnie got the chair ya'll better open up shop!

Both are right! Everyone should get off their ass and create the life they want for themselves, but as a child that grew up in poverty, I didn't know what was available and many people I knew didn't believe they were capable.

No man is an island. We all need a "hand up" instead of a "hand out".

So financially, I'm probably a Black Republican, but ethically I'm a Democrat because I care about the people. But if you know me I'm also anti-government so it's weird!

Don't be like ~~niggas~~ who get a lil money and get a white chick then wanna come back on this side and tell us about how we need to recognize we all are one and love white people. Kanye. That's cool and all. I'm just saying I've **ABSOLUTELY NEVER** heard of a white "influencer" telling white people it's time to love Black people. It's absolutely absurd. That let's me know we're not all in the same game. We need to worry about ourselves first.
"The white man let the slaves go, but ya'll won't let the white man go…" ~ *Nonie B.*

Free Enterprise

In the grand scheme of things, we're all just humans. Then there are *"the haves"* and *"the have-nots"*. You have the charitable and the greedy. Then you have good and evil. Do you see where I'm going with this? In America, if you're not a capitalist, you're a consumer and that's really *"the bottom of the food chain"*.

Free Enterprise. An economic system in which private business operates in competition and largely free of state control.

I really didn't understand the concept until I went to the islands. They explained to me in a real tourist way, how people come to this country and make a killing and those of us who are from here are still poor because we don't really understand the concept. People in other countries *DREAM* of coming to America to *start a business!* That's why you see immigrant parents get so upset in the movies when their kids would rather go work somewhere than to take over the family business. My grandfather is not an immigrant; he's black (Aborigine) and he did the same thing when my uncle didn't want to take over the family business.

Why do you think it's always been so hard for Black people to get small business loans? Now why would this system finance your *EMPOWERMENT*? It's all connected. It's not hard now though so get in position.

I know we all can't be business owners. Someone has to be the janitor. Someone has to flip the burgers. Someone has to bag the groceries. Some people even love it. That's to be respected. But think about it this way. You start working as a teen or in college. You work until 65 and then what? You die? Nah. You gotta keep living and it requires money.

Or we can talk about how the average number of sources of income for millionaires used to be 5, now it's 7. They have 7 sources of income and you're going to work 1 job for 40 years and not have any type of "side hustle"? That's how the rich get richer and the poor get poorer. The least you can do is take your income tax money and invest in the stock market or a small business. Make your money work for you. Ya'll pool money for the lottery.

Once you change tax brackets you realize the only color that matters is GREEN! Not saying there aren't millionaire and billionaire racists. I'm saying, imagine how many white people don't even know the info in this book, yet they vote Republican and have a "superiority complex". It's a joke. They're technically supporting a system that is

116

against them, but it's their "skin folk" so they'll align with them. We have to be loyal to *"the culture"* like that.

President Lyndon B. Johnson once said, "*If you can convince the lowest white man he's better than the best colored man, he won't notice you're picking his pocket. Hell, give him somebody to look down on, and he'll empty his pockets for you.*"

Long story short, don't be like the lowest of white men. And don't be like the lowest of black people— don't "get money" and forget about your people. Get money and help "the people" or "get money with your people". We're stronger in numbers.

Reparations

Dear Black People,
You'll never be "free" until you have free enterprise…

Until we create or should I say *"REBUILD"* a community of black entrepreneurs our people will always be at a disadvantage. They'll continue to have applications thrown out because of how their names are spelled. Black people will continue to make 3 times less than their white counterparts.

Reparations. The making of amends for a wrong one has done, by paying money to or otherwise helping those who have been wronged.

Reparation is also defined as the act of "repairing" something. Black people have been calling for reparations since *"The Emancipation Proclamation"*, but I say let's do this for ourselves.

Martin Luther King, Jr. was killed after organizing *"The Poor People's Campaign".* It was okay for him to tell Black people to get out there and get their asses beat and not fight back, but once he started looking for the money he became a problem:

"I think it is necessary for us to realize that we have moved from the era of civil rights to the era of human rights... [W]hen we see that there must be a radical redistribution of economic and political power..."[27]

In December 1967, Rev. Dr. King announced the plan to bring together poor people from across the country for a new march on Washington. This march was to demand better jobs, better homes, better education—better lives than the ones they were living. Rev. Dr. Ralph Abernathy explained that the intention of the Poor People's Campaign of 1968 was to "dramatize the plight of America's poor of all races and make very clear that they are sick and tired of waiting for a better life."[27]

I guess he was right when he said, *"I fear I may have integrated my people into a burning house."*

Ever heard of W.I.C.? Well that was a direct copy of The Black Panther Party's *"Free Breakfast For Children"* program they started in our communities in the late 60's and 70's. Why? The same reason we need to take care of each other today— no one else will. Many Blacks believe the system is broken. No. It was never meant to work for you. It's working the way they planned.

Here's a list of some of the programs the Black Panther Party are credited for:

1. Benefit Counseling
2. Black Student Alliance
3. Child Development Center
4. Consumer Education Classes
5. Community Facility Use
6. Community Health Classes
7. Community Pantry (Free Food Program)
8. Drug/Alcohol Abuse Awareness Program
9. Disabled Persons Services/Transportation and Attendant
10. Employment Referral Service
11. Free Ambulance Program
12. Free Breakfast for Children Programs
13. Free Busing to Prisons Program
14. Free Clothing Program

118

15. Free Commissary for Prisoners Program
16. Free Dental Program
17. Free Health Clinics
18. GED Classes
19. Intercommunal Youth Institute (becomes OCS by 1975)
20. Junior and High School Tutorial Program[28]

I'm showing you this to let you know we always took care of our own. We have to get back to that. We have to get back to Tulsa. We know what we need in our communities. Only we can put it there. We can't expect anyone else to take care of us. It doesn't need to be loud. It starts with just teaching the kids the right thing. They'll carry it out for us.

Conspectus

I must point out, this book is about the "Things I Learned From White Folks", not about what *"they taught me"*. I had a seat at the table and as they talked "around me" and "over my head"— but I was paying attention. I "peeped game" and took mental notes then I did my own ***RESEARCH***!

You have to get the idea out of your head that someone is going to hold your hand and walk you through life. You have to get our of the headspace that you are owed something. Even if the we're owed, we're not being compensated so we have to make sure we find other ways to be compensated, like learning the tricks "they" use.

I realized most of it is ***HIDDEN IN PLAIN SIGHT***.

Do yourself a favor, read and re-read this book. Then ***IMPLEMENT IT***!

This is your 40 ACRES AND A MULE! This is your REPARATIONS!

This book scratches the surface and lays the foundation for all that you can build!

Go out and get what's yours' cause them white folks over there getting rich, yet white women are the highest percentage of welfare recipients. It's insane! Oh, but *YOUR* riches are in "Heaven". Wake up Black people. It's **Game Time**. They're getting rich and hiding the money or "giving it away" to charities owned by family and friends, or themselves.

It's totally okay to live a humble life. We all should value the things in life that are FREE because they are the most important. We all should plant gardens. We all should give back to the less fortunate (old clothes, food or just time). These acts bring a richness to your life that money can't.

But what should we do about the rest of life, since nothing else is free? Get money and make sure your credit it right. Money can't buy happiness, but I'm sure it could buy a lot of things to make you happy.

Having money won't fix everything, but I'm sure money could fix about 80% of the problems you have right now. Don't hate money and don't hate on money. Just learn how to make it work for you.

You can wait until you get to heaven to enjoy your riches or you can live a **RICH LIFE** now.

Three months ago I was in St. Kitts watching the news. They were saying America is mad because they *"know"* over $1 billion is being hidden in Swiss banks on the sister island Nevis- **allegedly. You could allegedly do it too. Haha!**

See I'm going too far. If I continue this book will be over 300 pages. I'll continue that and more in my next book. We'll even talk about the *straw man and unclaimed property*. Stick with me and pretty soon your whole life and leisure will be a *"business expense"*— business owner humor! Laughing my ass off. That's money talk.

Remember the confusion surrounding billionaire presidential candidate (at the time), Donald Trump's tax returns?

How do you make $380 million in a year and not pay taxes? I figured it out. Now I'm going to do it. Your move...

The revolution will not be televised... but it will be read about.

And the next generations will say they learned this shit from a BLACK WOMAN!

References

1. **Eddie Griffin Talk About Foolish** https://www.youtube.com/watch?v=rmpoVV95BU0&t=902s

2. **40 Facts About Two Parent Families** https://www.yourazlawfirm.com/40-facts-two-parent-families/

3. **J. COLE "MONEY"** https://youtu.be/eKvlClFIJLo

4. **Dr. Nadine Burke "How Does Trauma Affect A Child's DNA?"** https://www.npr.org/templates/transcript/transcript.php?storyId=545092982

5. **Yoga** https://en.wikipedia.org/wiki/Yoga

6. **What Are Affirmations?** https://www.successconsciousness.com/affirmations.htm

7. **21 Affirmations To Transform Your** Lifehttp://dailycupofyoga.com/2016/02/06/21-affirmations-to-transform-your-life/

8. *Jesse Williams Speech BET Awards 2016* *http://time.com/4383516/jesse-williams-bet-speech-transcript/*

9. *How To Create A Budget* *https://www.wikihow.com/Create-a-Budget*

10. *Self growth.com*

11. **Ben Carson Says Poverty Is A 'State Of Mind'** *https://www.clasp.org/press-room/news-clips/ben-carson-says-poverty-state-mind*

12. *Keeping Up With The Joneses* *https://en.wikipedia.org/wiki/Keeping_up_with_the_Joneses*

13. *The 3 Credit Bureaus* *https://www.creditkarma.com/credit-cards/i/three-credit-bureaus/*

14. **10 questions to ask before getting a secured credit card** *https://www.bankrate.com/finance/credit-cards/10-questions-before-getting-a-secured-credit-card-1.aspx*

15. **Choosing Life Insurance: The Facts You're Missing** *https://www.trustedchoice.com/life-insurance/coverage-basics/whole-life-vs-term-life/*

16. **The Reading Habits of Ultra-Successful People** *https://www.huffingtonpost.com/andrew-merle/the-reading-habits-of-ult_b_9688130.html*

17. ***Rich Dad, Poor Dad*** *http://www.lequydonhanoi.edu.vn/upload_images/Sách%20ngoại%20ngữ/Rich%20Dad%20Poor%20Dad.pdf*

18. **6 Job Personality and Work Environment Types** *http://sourcesofinsight.com/6-personality-and-work-environment-types/*

19. **CRIMINAL JUSTICE FACT SHEET** *http://www.naacp.org/criminal-justice-fact-sheet/*

20. ***How Black Millennials Can Practice Group Economics*** *https://blavity.com/heres-a-few-ways-that-black-millennials-can-practice-group-economics-right-now*

21. **Mutual Fund** https://www.investopedia.com/terms/m/mutualfund.asp#ixzz56vmlVvr6

22. **The 15 Biggest Mergers Of All Time** https://finance.yahoo.com/news/15-biggest-mergers-time-175152979.html

23. **African Proverbs** Afritorial.com

24. **Bankruptcy Basics** http://www.uscourts.gov/services-forms/bankruptcy/bankruptcy-basics

25. **Gerrymandering** https://en.wikipedia.org/wiki/Gerrymandering

26. **Rapper 2 Chainz Campaigns for the Voting Rights of Convicted Felons** https://

www.hollywoodreporter.com/earshot/2-chainz-campaigns-voting-rights-384436

27. **Dr. King's Vision: The Poor People's Campaign of 1967-68** https://www.poorpeoplescampaign.org/index.php/poor-peoples-campaign-1968/

28. **WIC Program Was Originally Started by The Black Panther Party** http://countercurrentnews.info/2016/09/wic-program-started-black-panter-party/

29842435R00068